MAESTRO
Conductor or Metro-Gnome?

For Braham
who observed my 'pilgrim's progress' from afar.

MAESTRO
Conductor or Metro-Gnome?
Reflections from the Rostrum

MYER FREDMAN

sussex
ACADEMIC
PRESS

BRIGHTON • PORTLAND

Copyright © Myer Fredman 2006

The right of Myer Fredman to be identified as author of this work has been asserted in accordance with the Copyright, Designs and Patents Act 1988.

2 4 6 8 10 9 7 5 3 1

First published 2006 in Great Britain by
SUSSEX ACADEMIC PRESS
PO Box 2950
Brighton BN2 5SP

and in the United States of America by
SUSSEX ACADEMIC PRESS
920 NE 58th Ave   Suite 300
Portland, Oregon 97213-3786

All rights reserved. Except for the quotation of short passages for the purposes of criticism and review, no part of this publication may be reproduced, stored in a retrieval system, or transmitted, in any form or by any means, electronic, mechanical, photocopying, recording or otherwise, without the prior permission of the publisher.

British Library Cataloguing in Publication Data
A CIP catalogue record for this book is available from the British Library.

Library of Congress Cataloging-in-Publication Data
Fredman, Myer.
   Maestro, conductor or metro-gnome? : reflections from
  the rostrum / by Myer Fredman.
   p. cm.
   Includes bibliographical references (p.) and index.
   ISBN 1-84519-124-2 (p/b : alk. paper)
   1. Conducting. 2. Conductors (Music) I. Title.

ML458.F74 2006
781.45—dc22

                                    2005017690

Typeset and designed by G&G Editorial, Brighton & Eastbourne
Printed and bound by TJ International, Padstow, Cornwall
This book is printed on acid-free paper.

Contents

Prelude	vii
Acknowledgements	viii

The Craft that Precedes Art

Hearing is believing!	6
Scoring points	7
Baton, bludgeon or paintbrush?	12
Health	13

Roads to the Rostrum

Five minutes or a lifetime?	16
In the driver's seat	18
Selecting a Musical Director	21
Have baton will travel	22
Le chef d'orchestre	23
Pre-rehearsal rehearsal	24
Facing the inevitable	26
Close encounters	29
Applause, the audience and other critics	32
The metro-gnome: Conductor, Maestro	33

In the Theatre

The operatic microcosm	35
The General Manager	35
The Music Director	36
The Singer	37

Opera production	37
The baton in the pit	39

Janus on the Podium

Metamorphosis	41
At the crossroads	44

A Personal Pilgrim's Progress

The wand of youth	47
Cockaigne calling	50
Sojurn in Sussex	53
The Athens of the South	78
A new life begins	90
Coming full circle	96

Postlude

Table of equivalent note values	97
How fast is slow?	98
Dancing on the rostrum	100
What's in a name?	103
What does . . . mean?	103
Sources of quotations	114
Further books of interest	117
Index	118

Prelude

As a direct result of television and video, we can now observe a conductor's gestures and facial expressions as never before. Yet when Rimsky Korsakov observed Berlioz conducting during the French composer's Russian tour, his comment was that *'conducting is a mystery'*. This fact became evident to me when I assisted Otto Klemperer on his recording of Mozart's *Così fan tutte*. Neither I nor members of the orchestra with whom I talked in the coffee breaks had any doubt that they performed as Klemperer intended, despite his extraordinary gestures. Sir Charles Mackerras defined the art of conducting in one succinct sentence: *'I reckon that a good conductor can achieve almost anything by his <u>emanation</u>, providing the orchestra he works with is sensitive.'* Since that interview, a number of female conductors have knocked down the walls of what was once a chauvinistic domain to great effect, but the mystery and how it emanates will surely remain as long as the art and craft of conducting continues.

Looking back on my own career, I must have begun as a 'metrognome' and only later evolved into a conductor. It is my firm belief that the superlative – Maestro – should be reserved for a Toscanini, Walter, Beecham, Furtwängler or an Abbado, despite that title being used for any Tom, Dick or flash Harry. What follows is a distillation of observation and personal experience for the interest and occasional amusement of those wanting an insight into the world of conducting, which includes many facets of the profession that aspiring maestri will also find valuable.

Myer Fredman
Tasmania, August 2005

Acknowledgments

The author and publisher wish to acknowledge with thanks permission to reproduce the following photographs:

Page 56: A *Così fan tutte* production rehearsal on the Glyndebourne stage, 1969. Courtesy of Helen Gravett.

Page 87: *Let's Make an Opera*, 1979 and Midsummer Marriage, 1978. Both pictures by kind permission of The State Opera of South Australia.

Page 92: Camera rehearsal for an ABC television programme; rehearsing of *Vier Letzte Lieder* (Four Last Songs) with Elizabeth Söderström, 1984. Both pictures courtesy of Gordon Clarke Music in Camera Australia).

Page 93: In conference with Sir Charles Mackerras and Neil Flottmann; rehearsing the Sydney Symphony Orchestra. Both pictures courtesy of Gordon Clarke Music in Camera Australia.

MAESTRO
Conductor or Metro-Gnome?

Reflections from the Rostrum

The Craft that Precedes Art

The art as distinct from the craft is certainly a mystery because it stems from the innermost recesses of the heart and mind – the soul – fused in the crucible of the composer's imagination during a performance of an inspiring conductor. The craft is the means by which all three – the metro-gnome, the conductor and the maestro are able – in varying degrees, to externalise what they have absorbed from the printed page and heard with their inner ear.

A contributor to *Musical Opinion* (London 1890) had this to say about conductors, though he probably did so with his tongue set firmly in his cheek:

'The definition of a conductor is a man who describes forms in the air with a stick or wand and who expects, nay demands – all those before him to be subject and subordinated to him. He is the one man who produces nothing musically but claims to produce all things. "The band and the chorus are the instrument on which I play". Is this claim true or false? Can a band or a chorus do without him? Is the conductor only a self-elected acrobat who has cajoled a number of persons to believe in his assumed necessity? Is conducting the resort of those who have no speciality as instrumental or vocal performers? Is, in short, a conductor an ass in the lion's skin? The conductor is a useless excrescence of quite modern growth, nay he is worse, namely a detriment and not an advantage, and the musical world would be considerably benefited by his removal. Is the conductor a modern sinecure? Is not the very root and foundation of conducting based on the false premise – namely, that it is more natural for people to go isolated and in opposition and in antagonistic directions than for them to go together?'

All those before him to be subject and subordinated to him.
This was certainly true before musicians had full employment when the trade union movement had not yet come into existence. In

this more egalitarian age with artistic committees from within the orchestras, conductors have had to learn to be – sometimes the hard way – the first among equals. At best they respect the players as colleagues rather than as subordinates. At worst – the relationship is a benevolent dictatorship.

He is the one man who produces nothing musically but claims to produce all things.

The 'production' is surely in the quality of the emanation. Sir Charles Mackerras has alluded to the necessity of a sensitive orchestra in this respect.

The band and the chorus are the instrument on which I play.

The use of the word band rather than orchestra now seems decidedly patronising even derogatory but some conductors do 'play on top of' the orchestra like an organist on a number of keyboards and pedals: literally pulling out all the stops!

Can a band or a chorus do without him?

This was actually attempted soon after the revolution in Russia but as *'all pigs are equal only some are more equal than others'* (George Orwell's *Animal Farm*), it was soon realised that someone had to indicate the tempo in order to begin. It became the Concert Master's responsibility: at first he stood to be seen, then he was moved to a more central position on the rostrum, and thereby the conductor was surreptitiously re-instated. The short answer to the question therefore is that a conductor is necessary depending on the nature and complexity of the score.

Is conducting the resort of those who have no speciality as instrumental or vocal performers?

Many conductors start out as instrumentalists and a few graduate from being singers, but there is no reason why a non-executant cannot become a conductor though a pianistic ability is a distinct advantage. For an aspiring conductor to 'tread the boards' is also invaluable to discover what it means to be an actor or a singer and to face the public in the vast expanse of an auditorium. During my student days, for instance, I helped to burn Ingrid Bergman at the stake in a stage version of Honegger's *Jeanne d'Arc au Bûcher*, which incidentally helped to pay the rent!

Is the conductor a modern sinecure?

Jet-setting conductors certainly earn more than the man in the street though probably not as much as the average footballer or cricket star. On the other hand, considerable expense is incurred when buying scores, tail suits and the paraphernalia of the wandering minstrel even during the early stages of a career when engagements are few and far between.

Is not the very root and foundation of conducting based on the false premise – namely, that it is more natural for people to go isolated and in opposition and in antagonistic directions than for them to go together?

A strange assumption and it *'ain't necessarily so'* to quote Ira and George Gershwin.

A more constructive overview appeared in the *Boston Herald* a year after the above article was published:

'The conductor of the modern orchestra has a manifold task. First of all to know the technical drill which is the most wearing of all. The ruling of a band of sensitive musicians is in itself not an easy matter. To repress an enthusiastic cellist and cause him to subordinate his phrases to a viola passage which he considers of minor importance, or to subdue an over zealous trombonist, is not a trifling thing to do. But before even this is done, the conductor's work has begun; and he has carefully studied the score so that he may have a clear idea of what he intends to do. There is generally an antagonism between the strict conductor and his men, the former desiring too much rehearsal, the latter too little. The discipline of an orchestra should be as rigid as that of a military company and the distinctions *of rank are almost as fixed; it is a matter of infinite importance to the musician whether he sits in the front row or the second, or at the fifth desk or the tenth.*

The ideal conductor must not only feel the emotion of a work, but he must be able to express it to his men, by words at rehearsals, by gesture at the concert. The beating of the time is very important, as an indecisive beat will cause the attack to be irregular. Many composers sin in this respect, and cannot conduct their own works with nearly as good results as are achieved by the trained conductor. The signalling of the different entrances of the instruments is another task of the conductor. If the kettle drums have fifty-seven measures rest, they should count them, and know exactly when they are to resume playing; but as a matter of fact, they rest with calm tranquillity on the shoulders of the conductor, and rely on him to give them the signal to play the first notes of their phrase. These are a few of the chief duties of a modern orchestral conductor. To those who imagine that to shake a stick rhythmically over an orchestra is to lead it, may seem exaggerated. Meanwhile when one sees a gentleman in the rural districts swelling with importance because he is shaking the stick in question, and determined to get six entire shakes into each measure of a six-eight movement, or die, we can but recall the term applied to those conductors in Europe; they are called Metro-gnomes.'

The ruling of a band of sensitive musicians is in itself not an easy matter.

This is very true as the psychology of rehearsing is as important as technical ability; some believe even more so. Likewise an instinctive verbal ability is necessary to clearly express one's intentions. Woodwind players, for instance, often have exposed and challenging solos and they are sensitive – sometimes hypersensitive – to a badly chosen word from the rostrum.

There is generally an antagonism between the strict conductor and his men, the former desiring too much rehearsal, the latter too little.

Some orchestral musicians profess that they would rather be elsewhere than at the rehearsal but when the conductor respects the players' musicality, orchestras willingly respond. A classic example was when Rudolf Kempe started to rehearse *Tristan und Isolde* at 10 A.M. on the morning after a very demanding première the previous night. Sensing their exhaustion he soon stopped and said *'the rest is perfect, good morning ladies and gentlemen'*; they responded accordingly with a subsequent intensely moving performance.

> *The discipline of an orchestra should be as rigid as that of a military company and the distinctions of rank are almost as fixed; it is a matter of infinite importance to the musician whether he sits in the front row or the second, or at the fifth desk or the tenth.*

The word discipline (synonym for self-control) is unfashionable at the moment but there has always been — and hopefully there will always need to be — discipline in its proper meaning, for an orchestra depends on the merging of the player's individual self-control to work towards their common goal. This is totally different from parade ground discipline and though most of the former rigid formalities have been relaxed, respect for each other's importance in the ensemble remains essential. Seating, however, is a problem as a string player may object to sitting with an incompatible colleague while the brass section — who often have periods of inactivity in pre-Romantic music — may easily become restless, which then permeates through the whole orchestra. As Bruno Walter wrote in his book *Of Music and Music Making*:

> *'His is the will, theirs the obligation, and as passive obligation is also de-personalization which cannot yield artistic results, the conductor must be able to persuade the musicians and they be transformed into willing participants . . . An adequate degree of external discipline is as indispensable in the artistic workshop as cleanliness and orderliness are in a well-run household . . . there is a danger in the power that the conductor wields. It is in his interests as a human being as much as a conductor to resist the temptation to use it. Intimidation deprives the musician of the full enjoyment of his talents. Yet sometimes it is necessary to be severe in certain circumstances, even indispensable.'*

It becomes a matter of degree as to how, where and when to draw the line.

The ideal conductor must not only feel the emotion of a work, but he must be able to express it to his men, by words at rehearsals, by gesture at the concert.

Ideally this sentence should read *gesture* first and *words* second even during a rehearsal and then, only as a last resort. There is a saying that a conductor's power to communicate is in inverse proportion to his or her ability to talk. Talkative conductors can bore the pants off an orchestra though having a talent for verbal pictures is a valuable asset even if it is difficult to find the right words in the heat of the moment. Sir Adrian Boult hardly ever spoke during a rehearsal except to say something like *'Good morning ladies and gentlemen, let us rehearse Elgar's* First Symphony' at the beginning, and *'Thank you very much, that was splendid'* at the end.

Hearing is believing

Musicians may envy colleagues who have what is termed absolute pitch – knowing the pitch of a note instinctively without having to play it – but it may also be a handicap as the slightest deviation can literally cause earache and physical discomfort. This is illustrated by a story about Brahms who spent an uncomfortable evening at a dinner party because the lady on his right talked in F major while the lady on his left talked in E minor. Obviously an accurate ear is the foremost requirement for any musician but even more so for a conductor who has to instantly recognise a wrong note or an unbalanced chord. One ambitious young conductor deliberately altered the printed note in the second trombone part from a C to a B in a very loud passage so as to impress the players with his acute ear. Arriving at that bar in the rehearsal he stopped and with great aplomb, pointed out that the second trombonist was playing a B instead of a C. *"Oh no"*, the player called out, *"I know perfectly well that it should be a C but some silly idiot altered my part."*

The conductor's bluff had been called in one fell swoop: a salutary lesson! Honesty should always be the best policy, as Sir Thomas Beecham rightly knew when his memory deserted him and the orchestra ground to a halt. He turned round and addressed the audience *'Ladies and Gentlemen, there appears to be a hiatus, I propose to begin again'*, which he then proceeded to do! When (rather than if) a conductor makes a mistake, it should be admitted quite openly as players are immediately aware of any camouflage. *'When you get lost, and you will, everybody does at one time or another, just make some elegant vague motion and we'll put it all to rights quickly enough'* was the gratuitous advice given to one conductor. Being only human, conductors do make mistakes. The Anglo-Irish composer Sir Charles Stanford proposed that batons should be manufactured with bells attached at the point so that whenever a conductor errs, it automatically rings. Should such a baton ever be made, numberless orchestras would be deafened by the tintinnabulation!

Scoring points

Obviously a pre-requisite for any conductor is a thorough knowledge of composition: harmony (sound experienced vertically as chords), counterpoint (horizontally, in individual lines), figured bass (the numerical shorthand for harmony) and fugue (the permutations of a theme). Lorin Maazel mentioned that he even had to compose a fugue a day for an entire year in his student days. From such studies, conductors learn about the flow of music and how phrases grow into one another to create paragraphs and chapters, or in musical terms, complete movements. A conductor is therefore akin to an architect's assistant who sees that the design takes shape as intended by the composer. Orchestration of all periods – from early to modern – has also to be studied as it has changed a great deal over the centuries. There are many books on the subject: Richard Strauss' revision of the *Treatise on Instrumentation* by Hector Berlioz being arguably the most comprehensive.

Whereas instrumentalists read a single line, and keyboard players, two, orchestral scores may contain up to thirty lines and occasionally more. Indeed, until the nineteenth century the treble instruments were at the top of the page, the bass instruments at the bottom and the middle instruments in between. More recently the format has changed and scores are now laid out according to their 'families', read downwards as follows:

The woodwind instruments braced together at the top of the page consisting basically of flutes, oboes, clarinets, and bassoons with the horns on a separate stave below.
The brass instruments including trumpets, cornets, trombones and tuba.
The timpani on its own stave and the percussion on as many as needed for the bass drum, side drum, cymbals and countless other struck and plucked instruments.
The harp(s) with two staves like a piano.
Solo instruments, singers and/or choir need as many as twelve staves under the harp but are sometimes printed between the violas and cellos.
The strings occupy the lowest brace of staves in which the 1st. and 2nd Violins are bracketed together and underneath them, the violas, cellos and double-basses.

A score is as much a pictorial image of sound as is the printed word in a book, the difference being that in a book a page consists of single lines whereas in a score there are many lines and each is read both horizontally and vertically *at the same time*. Another difference is that orchestral scores include transposing instruments that are printed in one key but sound in another because of their basic construction. The transposing instruments are the clarinets, with different mouthpieces for different keys and the horns and trumpets that at one time had to change their crooks for different keys; but with the invention of the valve, virtually any key became possible. Curiously the French horn isn't specifically French and though made of brass it was at one time classified as a woodwind instrument. Other transposing instruments are the alto flute and cor anglais (neither English nor a horn); and the piccolo sounds an octave higher than written (at one time written in G); while the double bass and contra bassoon sound an octave lower. Orchestral scores also have a number of clefs other than those used by keyboard players, the alto clef for the violas, the tenor clef for the cellos, bassoons (sometimes) and trombones, and the soprano clef which is still in evidence in older editions of pre-nineteenth century music. Not so long ago, a number of composers began to write their scores with the clarinet, horn and trumpet parts printed as sounding rather than transposed and some scores by Prokofiev and Samuel Barber even have the horn and cor anglais parts in the alto rather than the treble clef. Such scores can be very disconcerting for those conductors trained to subconsciously transpose and are thrown off balance as a result. Fortunately the fashion of only printing the bars that are actually played by that particular instrument, leaving vast blank spaces on the page, has gone the way of all flesh as bar lines had to be painstakingly drawn down every page in order to see the alignment.

Conductors should have at least a working knowledge of virtually every orchestral instrument as it is only right and proper that whoever stands in front of an orchestra knows something about their capabilities. Long and short strokes in string playing affect dynamics and articulation: whether to play tremolo (very fast reiteration of the bow) or measured thirty-second notes (demisemiquavers): vibrato, portato, louré, flautato, detaché, spiccato, martellato and harmonics. In the woodwind family, the flutes have no reeds, clarinets have one, oboes, cor anglais and bassoons have two, so intonation problems arise that have to be resolved by the conductor. Sir Henry Wood even had a machine constructed that emitted an "A" to which every player tuned before going onto the platform; nowadays there is an electronic equivalent which no player can fault. Horns are played 'open' or bouché (stopped), cuivré (a forced ringing tone) or coperto, the latter appearing in several modern scores to baffle some horn players as well as conductors! In fact Mozart used the term for the timpani, meaning that the player should 'cover' the sound by muting it with a piece of cloth. A few modern composers have adopted this idea in their horn writing with the Trombone Concerto by Sirocco and Poulenc's *Dialogues des Carmélites* being two examples. *Schalltrichter auf* (French: *Pavillon dan l'air*) means that the bell of the horn has to be lifted up over the shoulders but players usually refrain from doing so until the concert itself as it is extremely tiring on their lips as well as their arms. The ophicleide was a brass instrument favoured by Berlioz, Wagner and Mendelssohn but it is now obsolete and usually replaced by a tuba or contra-bassoon. The cimbasso has also disappeared so the tuba is substituted (wrongly) when some of Verdi's earlier operas are revived. The tuba really came into its own with Britten who, in his *Spring Symphony*, *Peter Grimes*, and *Death in Venice*, used it brilliantly for dramatic purposes, especially in the latter opera in which it symbolises the cholera infecting Venice!

The percussion department was considerably enlarged during the twentieth century and now includes such exotic instruments as the anvil, the whip, antique cymbals (Debussy's *L'après-midi d'un faune*), vibraphone, sandpaper and a whole phalanx of weird and wonderful instruments. A knowledgeable conductor knows that to make a good sound on the Gran Cassa (bass drum) the player needs to 'prime' the instrument before playing it; similarly the conductor needs to know the different sound of the vibraphone's motor when tuned on or off, and the sound qualities of different types of mallet. Britten revelled in the percussion department in many of his works and in *Death in Venice* had five percussion players to simulate a Balinese gamelan orchestra as well as a tuned drum, two whips, a wind-machine, a bell-tree and crotales. Arnold Bax employed an anvil in his *Third Symphony* and Havergal Brian wrote for an inordinate number of snare drums! Conductors are often asked whether a timpani part of the classical era should be played as a roll or as thirty-seconds (demi-semiquavers) but percussion parts are now meticulously written out in every possible (and impossible) rhythmic permutation. Conductors should also understand harp-pedalling notation as exemplified in many of the scores of Debussy and Ravel.

The Saxophone has become a standard orchestral instrument having been exploited by Saint-Saëns, Bizet, Debussy, and more recently Milhaud and Vaughan-Williams to name just a few. Richard Strauss wrote for the euphonium in *Don Quixote* and *Ein Heldenleben* and Debussy the oboe d'amore in *Gigues*. Delius used a sarrusophone (the contra-bassoon is an alternative) in his *Song of the High Hills* and *A Dance Rhapsody* and a bass oboe in his *Requiem*, though his most bizarre request was in *Eventyr*. The men in the orchestra had to give a wild shout of *Hei* not once but twice and *ffff* (probably because women weren't allowed into orchestras in his time).

Some composers have deliberately written off the compass of the instrument so that the players can sense the totality of the phrase in question. Richard Strauss took the violins down to an F, a whole tone below its lowest note, and Britten took the Piccolo to one note below its normal range in *Billy Budd*. Sibelius did likewise for the flute towards the end of *Tapiola*, possibly because the flautist in the Helsinki orchestra could play it.

Not all conductors need to mark their scores while others go to the other extreme of using different coloured pencils to highlight individual entries or the various instrumental families. Playing the score on the piano confirms the accuracy of the inner ear for those without the gift of absolute pitch while the mental and finger dexterity involved in encompassing a chord from the top to the bottom of the page, helps to develop the memory. Even if it is painfully slow at first playing the printed page rather than listening to recordings, this exercise remains the shortest distance between creator and re-creator as Wagner well knew when he copied out Beethoven's entire *Choral Symphony* to enhance his understanding of that work.

Having a keyboard facility is also a practical advantage for the aspiring conductor because it provides an opening into the profession as a repetiteur which in turns opens up a path to the rostrum. Bruno Walter was an excellent pianist as well as a great conductor who maintained that participation in chamber music was invaluable not only to open the eyes and ears to a whole world of music, but also to encourage a harmonious relationship with fellow musicians. He also believed that fine art and philosophy are equally important for a complete human being and consequently for the art of conducting. His observation is still very pertinent as not all conductors think about matters beyond their immediate concern. Walter was in fact reiterating the philosophy of both the medieval philosopher Boethius who believed that the highest form of music existed in the body and soul in perfect harmony, and Augustine who was convinced that music purified the soul.

Baton, bludgeon or paint brush?

The use of a baton is purely a matter of personal preference as such eminent conductors as Pierre Boulez can testify; for them it is an unnatural and impersonal stick, while for others it is a magic wand with which to cast a spell! This was certainly the case with Sir Thomas Beecham who quipped *'it's easy, all you have to do is waggle a stick'*. The early conductors banged the floor with a mace to indicate the pulse until the seventeenth-century Italian/French composer Lully died of gangrene having mistakenly banged his toe. Thereafter the baton was gradually adopted for reasons of longevity. However, they can still be lethal especially when made from fibreglass, for they easily shred and get under the skin or flick out of the hand and can easily pierce the eye of an unlucky player. One conductor deliberately broke his (wooden) baton to show his displeasure at the orchestra while another – who always insisted on being addressed as *maestro* (unwarranted) – rebuked his assistant for putting out his 'Tchaikovsky baton' when he was about to conduct a Beethoven symphony.

The first recorded use of a baton was in 1820 when Louis Spohr conducted in London, where it was still the custom for the conductor to sit at the piano. *'The orchestra of the London Philharmonic Society was spread over a vast platform, and unanimity was out of the question in spite of the excellence of individual players. I therefore determined to remedy this defective system. I produced a baton from my pocket and gave the signal to begin. The novelty aroused their attention and, helped by seeing the time beaten out clearly, the players performed with a spirit and correctness unknown previously. The baton triumphed and no conductor was seen again at the piano in an orchestral work.'*

Health

With so much travel and hectic rehearsal schedules required of conductors today, physical health is vitally important yet some seem unconcerned about their physical well-being, relying perhaps on the myth that conductors are by nature, long-lived. This is true to a certain extent but those that die young are soon forgotten, having had little opportunity to make an impression on the musical world. Conducting may appear to be beneficial to health simply as physical exercise (though chiefly the upper torso), but if conductors gesticulated for as long as a symphony without its musical stimulus, it would surely result in serious heart problems or worse! Considerable energy is required to rehearse and perform that can also create the problem of an inordinate craving for food and drink (often late at night) that again is decidedly unhealthy. Good posture is vital because conductors spend many hours standing and because it is the basis on which the conductor's body language expresses his or her complete personality to which orchestral players instinctively respond. Standing for such long periods, especially when conducting opera, creates tremendous pressure on the legs and feet and can cause cardio-vascular problems so I often stood on one foot and wagged the other, to the amusement of the musicians. Another result of the physical involvement is the amount of perspiration exuded during the course of any one rehearsal or performance.

One conductor was alleged to fail his students if they sweated just one drop and Richard Strauss advised young conductors that they ought not to perspire but the public should become warm.

The physical and mental stresses involved in conducting was the subject of a research project carried out by The Institute of Fitness in Adelaide, South Australia, during the 1970s. The subjected conductor was examined before and during rehearsals, culminating in a performance of Dvořák's *Eighth Symphony*, which is perhaps not as long or physically or as emotionally stressful as a symphony by Mahler or Shostakovitch. The results stated that the 1st CONDITION was a low stress period with the conductor alone in an air-conditioned studio preparing for the rehearsal. The 2nd CONDITION was during the orchestral rehearsal in their studio and the final rehearsal in the concert hall was of moderate stress while the 3rd CONDITION, during the performance was the highest period of stress. During the 1st CONDITION, he experienced minimal stress but during the 2nd and 3rd CONDITIONS his cardio-vascular demands increased. The physical exercise having only contributed a little to the two- and three-fold increments over the resting heart rate during the 2nd CONDITION, though his starting heart rate was 30 beats higher than the peak of the 1st CONDITION. The research showed that the elevated heart-rates during the rehearsals and concert were from psycho-social stress augmented during the performance by the weight and heat of his heavier tail suit, contributing to the highest rate of all.

The cardio-vascular load sustained during the symphony (over 30 minutes) was considerable and the conductor would no doubt have experienced a similar situation on a fairly regular weekly basis during the course of a year The considered opinion therefore was that *'conducting an orchestra is a very stressful occupation but for most conductors it is a desirable form of stress which subsides when the activity is completed. It may explain why, in part, conductors often live long lives and it may also be due to their love for, and dedication to, the profession, which is a well-established recipe for good health.*

Another important factor is the emotional satisfaction which musicians presumably gain from an intense appreciation of their art and associated sensory stimulations. However, the lives of musicians and conductors are not all beer and skittles but they are fortunate in having perhaps a nice balance between the good and the bad, the source of the good being music!'

Hearing loss is now generally accepted as part of the ageing process but musicians have even greater cause for concern because it can affect their means of livelihood. During the loudest passages in *Madame Butterfly* and *Turandot,* for instance – of which there are quite a few – some players in the Sydney Opera House have to plug their ears and the Bayreuth pit also has a decibel problem, as testified by musicians who have spent many hours there. As electronically amplified pop music now invades virtually every moment of the day hearing loss now occurs three times faster than previously, and as conductors seem to encourage greater volume and percussive accents than previously, their own loss has been accelerated along with that of the players. Having reached such alarming proportions the Association of British Orchestras warned its players a few years ago that under recent European noise regulations, it might become unlawful to perform loud passages. This led to one musician's comment that as in Bruckner's *Eighth Symphony* the brass actually produces more decibels than Concorde taking off, many nineteenth and twentieth century scores would have to be banned should this regulation be enforced! The use of a hearing aid is obviously the answer though the general assumption exists that a conductor's ability to distinguish an error in the music is affected is certainly not the case. The loss only affects the highest frequencies and the consonants *b, d, k, p, s,* and *t,* and little else so the problem usually occurs only when players at the back of the orchestra ask questions and fail to project their voices. The percussionist Evelyn Glennie solved the problem incredibly well and isn't afraid to publicise her 'disability', so conductors and players alike ought to use the latest technology to correct the misconception that hearing loss automatically jeopardises a musician's right to work.

Roads to the Rostrum
Five minutes or a lifetime?

A number of illustrious maestri have maintained that conducting can't be taught at all. Others believe that it only takes five minutes to learn. Both views confuse the art with the craft. If singers and instrumentalists have teachers and instruments on which to practice why should aspiring conductors be denied expert tuition even though they have no orchestra on which to practice. Exceptional talents – some with minimal technique – make an immediate impact on an orchestra but, as a general rule, the craft has to be initially mastered on a one-to-one basis with a teacher simulating the orchestra at the piano. In his *Handbook of Conducting*, Hermann Scherchen wrote that *'conducting should not be confused either with dramatic acting, pantomime, or gymnastics. Its ideal should be that no part of the body except the right arm should move. There is no need to resort to distorting emotional grimaces; on the contrary, the eyes should be kept free, alert and ready, for they must watch, help, indicate and encourage. It is only if a conductor is altogether free from constraint, and when his controlling energies are never cramped or distorted, that he is capable of carrying his orchestra to the utmost development of its power and getting the best from each player'*. Scherchen ought to have mentioned that eyebrows can also be used to great advantage as, by all accounts, Artur Nikisch and Richard Strauss were able to work wonders with them. But Furtwängler would not have been acceptable to Scherchen. When he was asked why he made such extraordinary gyrations to launch Mozart's *Don Giovanni* Overture his reply was that any conductor could give a clear down-beat but he wanted to create a climactic opening chord which he could only indicate that way. It used to be said about Furtwängler that orchestras knew when to begin when his hand reached the bottom stud on his shirt but only after seven rebounds. Another equally unfathomable conductor was scheduled to conduct Richard Strauss' *Don Juan*, which has a reputation for being difficult to set in motion. Before the conductor arrived, the leader told the assembled orchestra that whatever the conductor did when he reached the rostrum they should take as the signal to start. As the conductor stepped onto the rostrum he took out his handkerchief, blew his nose – and *Don Juan* burst into action!

The conductor's working area is the equivalent of a painter's canvas with the chin and navel being the horizontals and the sides of the body, the verticals varying according to individual physique. On this canvas the direction of the beat and tempo can then be painted with or without a baton and, continuing the painting metaphor, the right hand or baton becomes a paintbrush as it is psychologically more constructive for a student to think of painting rather than beating time. Then comes the complete range of dynamics, from *pianissimo* to *fortissimo* by rotating the fingers, then the wrist followed by the elbow and finally the full arm to encompass the smallest and largest possible circle. This ability is vitally important as orchestral musicians are often confused by the conductor's admonition that they are not playing softly enough, contradicted by the conductor's gesture obviously demanding them to play louder! Another basic ability to be absorbed and digested is that the left hand should be complimentary to the right and not its mirror image as duplication only halves the impact when the conductor should aim to achieve the maximum effect with the minimum of effort! The upturned palm of the left hand can be used to encourage, while down-turned – especially when the fingers are spread wide – conveys the opposite; it can also indicate a crescendo, a diminuendo, a precise staccato, and a broad legato. In opera the left hand is also used to cue the singers while the right hand guides the orchestra yet Richard Strauss, himself a very economical conductor, believed that *'The left hand has nothing to do with conducting, its proper place is in the waistcoat pocket from which it should emerge to restrain or make some minor gesture for which in any case, a scarcely imperceptible glance would suffice.'* Incidentally, orchestral players have no difficulty in understanding left-handed conductors despite gestures being the reverse. This confirms that a good conductor, whether left or right-handed, *emanates.*

In the driver's seat

After the basic gestures are thoroughly absorbed, the student's next step is to search for opportunities for practical experience, with the most readily available being amateur and/or student orchestras and choirs. The problem with most amateur orchestras is that being concerned with their own technical inadequacies they are unable to give much attention to anything other than finding the right notes and only occasionally sensing the conductor. This tends to create muscular tensions for the conductor, the very opposite to what he or she should be aiming – fluid gestures. Student orchestras are often more technically advanced so that a great deal can be learnt especially about the inevitable mistakes if a video camera is also used. The picture can then be viewed privately without the teacher's comments (even when constructive) being overheard by the orchestra as this is demeaning for the aspiring conductor. Conducting an amateur choir is an excellent way of developing eye to eye contact, communication using pictorial language and learning to breath instinctively, for as Wagner wrote *'Our conductors so frequently fail to find the real tempo because they are ignorant of singing. I have not yet to meet with a German Capellmeister who, be it with a good or bad voice, can really sing a melody. These people, look upon music as a singularly abstract sort of thing, an amalgam of grammar, arithmetic and digital gymnastics'*: summed up in one word, metrognomic! So the intake of breath, a natural instinct for all singers, is then externalised in the preparatory beat (up beat) and conveys the tempo without rigidity. Unfortunately, there is a prevalent attitude that choral music is less worthy of attention than the symphonic repertoire, but by working with a choir a fledgling conductor learns that symphonic music must also breathe if it is to be truly alive.

Young conductors should be allowed to mature at their own pace but they are often seduced by early successes or winning a competition, and then succumb to the surrounding hype and publicity. Some manage to consolidate their success and embark on brilliant careers but winning a competition can be destructive for a burgeoning talent especially if he or she is by nature a late developer. Many orchestras now run apprentice schemes that allow promising conductors to observe experienced practitioners and get the feel of a professional orchestra in rehearsal and performance (the two can be remarkably different). But having to quickly learn an extensive repertoire and at the same time handle a reluctant orchestra can undermine a blossoming talent so it's better if a young conductor makes haste slowly. It takes many years to be a success overnight! Mozart knew this when he wrote in English, *'Patience and tranquillity of mind contribute more to cure our distempers as the whole art of medicine'*.

Some conductors with private means buy their experience and in the 1950s they often presented all Tchaikovsky and all Beethoven programmes, but when they rehearsed the orchestras could impart little. One even told the orchestra that there was no need to rehearse the scherzo in Beethoven's A major Symphony (No. 7) because they knew it very well but he would observe the usual repeats. At the concert, chaos reigned because various players had observed different repeats under different conductors so consequently a mixture of the Scherzo in a flat key and the Trio in sharp key resounded round the auditorium! Sir Thomas Beecham also hailed from a wealthy family but was very much the exception, though he wasn't always taken seriously in the profession as a consequence. Most orchestras have players in their ranks that start out with an ambition to conduct but as the opportunity never arises they become bitter and take pot shots at whoever stands before them; others seize on every opportunity. Toscanini, Barbirolli (both cellists), Koussevitzky a double-bass player, Sir Colin Davis a clarinettist, Sir Neville Mariner a violinist, and Sir Charles Mackerras an oboist are just a few who have succeeded in crossing the divide, while Lorin Maazel, Daniel Barenboim and Vladimir Aschkenazy began as instrumental virtuosi.

The most well trodden path to the rostrum, however, remains that of the repetiteur in an opera company who has to play un-pianistic reductions of an opera's orchestral score and follow any number of conductors – an invaluable way of discovering what conducting is all about from the orchestra's perspective. Other responsibilities include coaching singers when learning new roles or revising familiar ones and having to cue in missing vocal lines at the same time as playing the piano part. Unfortunately musicians are not always blessed with beautiful voices or able to sing in tune so singers usually prefer their cues to be played rather than sung. Legend has it that the better the conductor, the less their vocal accomplishment and vice versa. By becoming a repetiteur, the drama inherent in all music is absorbed alongside ample opportunities to practice conducting backstage. This may range from a solitary horn in Act 3 of *Falstaff* to organ, drums and chorus in *I Puritani*, and a complete cafe orchestra in *Der Rosenkavalier*. The natural progression is then to conduct production rehearsals with piano, take sectional rehearsals with the orchestra and eventually performances, often with little or no rehearsal. This is an excellent test of *emanation* especially when faced with differing ways of conducting the same music such as the opening chords of the Overture to *Die Zauberflöte*. One conductor may indicate eight quavers and another four crotchets, some separate the chords while others play them in as tight a rhythm as possible alla Rossini. Having to stand in another's shoes is naturally restricting but succeeding usually means that opportunities then open up to become a fully-fledged conductor.

Female conductors were virtually unknown until the twentieth century as it was considered far too strenuous for a lady, yet paradoxically it was considered perfectly respectable to be a concert pianist. Then around the turn of the twentieth century they began to make an appearance with Dame Ethel Smyth, Avril Coleridge-Taylor and, nearer our own times, Imogen Holst, all proving to be good conductors. Now, thanks to the endeavours of a growing number of talented female conductors they are fully accepted in their own right by both orchestras and audiences. It is no longer a question of if homely they are not wanted and if beautiful too distracting as was previously the case. Daniel Barenboim's comment on Simone Young is more to the point in that she is unconcerned about being more masculine than her male colleagues, or exploits her feminine charms but prefers to concentrate on interpreting the music.

Selecting a Musical Director

A short list is drawn up from which the most likely candidates are invited to work as guest conductors for one or two concerts during which the players fill in a questionnaire as to whether they consider the candidate to be Excellent, Good, Fair, or Poor. The questions are usually along the following pattern.

Baton technique. How well does his baton technique indicate when and how he wants you to play? (cueing, preparatory beats, sub-division, dynamics, etc.).

Knowledge of the score. How thorough is his knowledge of the scores he has conducted?

Repertoire strengths. From your experience with this conductor, does he appear to have particular repertoire strengths in Pre-classical, Classical, Romantic, early 20th century, or Contemporary?

Musical style. How well do you feel he understands the various musical styles he has conducted?

Knowledge of the Orchestra. Evaluate his knowledge of the capabilities and special problems of your own instrumental group.

Rehearsal technique. Does he use time efficiently, communicate effectively with confidence and courtesy, and avoid wasted effort?

Leadership. Evaluate his leadership qualities. (Does he command the respect of the orchestra? Does the orchestra respond willingly?)

Re-Engagement. Would you like him to conduct our orchestra again? If this was his second or more visit, would you consider him a possible Chief or Principal Guest Conductor?

Subjective Response. Do you like him as a person? How do you think the concert(s) went?
General Comments.
Grading: 1–12 with 1 being the lowest and 12 the highest.

It is ostensibly a democratic procedure but it has been known for management to ignore the questionnaire and engage a Music Director for an ulterior motive such as having an extensive recording contract -- vitally important in today's economic climate. Having an extensive recording contract is not a foolproof guide, however, and whereas a first-rate conductor can inspire a second-rate orchestra to play better than they thought possible, a second-rate one (with such a contract) can reduce a first-class orchestra to third-class status. Nevertheless, a top-ranking orchestra never allows itself to perform below a certain standard regardless of who is standing on the rostrum.

Have baton will travel

A three-year contract has become the norm but it now implies well spaced-out visits each of approximately three to four weeks so the title 'permanent conductor' is now something of a misnomer. Conductors have created a problem for themselves in that if absent too long or too often, their residency is undermined, but if they accept a permanent contact in the previous meaning of the word they can lose a foothold on the international circuit! This situation has created a shuttle service between orchestras all over the world thanks to the ease of international air-travel. Indeed until the cancellation of Concorde it was actually possible to rehearse in New York and London on the same day! The life of a jet-setting conductor may seem to be exciting and glamorous to the layman, but constant travel, the same airport lounge in every city, jet lag, lonely hotel rooms and having to perpetually charm total strangers in endless receptions all take their toll. Hugo Wolf was already aware of this in the nineteenth century even if he never imagined it would grow to such proportions. *'One can be an excellent conductor and yet not at one with the orchestra which is not one's own, as for instance a virtuoso is with an instrument . . . An orchestra upon which conductor Mr. A has impressed the seal of his individuality in certain characteristics of rhythm, melody, in solo and ensemble playing, and a thousand other finesses, cannot in a few rehearsals be brought to a point where it interprets satisfactorily the intentions of another conductor, Mr. B, when it took years of effort on the part of Mr. A to accustom it to himself. To God alone are all things possible.'* In more recent times Mariss Janssons observed the corollary that *'when you are a guest conductor, someone else has made the soup and you get to eat the dessert . . . orchestras give honour and love to guest conductors, not to music directors'*.

Le chef d'orchestre

The planning of a programme is comparable to choosing a menu for a sumptuous banquet from many exotic recipes but the order in which they are served also requires careful thought. Wonderful overtures like Tchaikovsky's *Hamlet* or Elgar's *In the South* are longer than most others and are likely to overshadow the concerto that usually follows. The chef's *piece de resistance* in the banquet can also present a problem as masterpieces such as Schubert's *Unfinished*, Brahms' *Third Symphony* or Elgar's *Second Symphony* rarely receive rapturous applause, however lovingly they are performed: the reason being that their closing pages are so serene. A programme may reflect a conductor's penchant for a particular composer yet it can also pigeonhole a reputation. Sir Thomas Beecham was justifiably famous for his Mozart and Delius but he was equally superb in Berlioz, Debussy, Puccini, Sibelius, Richard Strauss and Wagner and a host of 'minor' composers, yet his name was always associated with the first two. Likewise Sir Charles Mackerras, a recognised authority for his Janácek and Czech music in general, is also a master interpreter of Wagner, Handel, and Sullivan and many others.

It is usual for more than one conductor to be engaged for a season, so their programmes must be complimentary for the orchestra as well as the audience in order to provide an interesting and balanced diet. Unfortunately, programmes seem to have adopted a rigid pattern of Overture/Concerto/Interval/Symphony albeit that attempts to rejuvenate this pattern have been made. One series included works all composed in the same year though markedly different in style so that Elgar's *Violin Concerto* shared a programme with Stravinsky's *Petrouchka*, and both were experienced with refreshing insight by orchestra and audience alike. A second format allowed the audience to participate in a weekend study of a Beethoven symphony with the conductor explaining points of interest along the way, concluding with a performance; and another included art exhibitions of the same period to illustrate the artistic ethos of the era. The promotion of new music also presents problems for, despite the many masterpieces of the last hundred years or so, modern music remains a box office nightmare. Conductors who valiantly crusade for it either devote an entire programme for an enthusiastic captive audience or are compelled to schedule it early in the concert to prevent a gradual exodus from the auditorium. Another grossly neglected repertoire is the genre known as 'light' music by such master composers as Saint-Saëns, Dvorák, Chabrier, Sibelius, Elgar, Massenet, Delibes and many others that Beecham conducted under the cheeky title of 'lollipops'. Most of such splendid works have vanished from symphonic programmes but their revival would attract new audiences as well as rejuvenate stereotyped programming.

*P*re-rehearsal rehearsal

Music is a language like any other with the equivalent of syllables, words, sentences, paragraphs and chapters so a perspicacious conductor digests every aspect of the work's outer and inner meaning be it tragic or triumphant, joyful or sad, thoughtful or frivolous. It was the composer's imagination that conjured up the work's *spirit* behind the printed page that is then organised by the conductor, but if he or she merely takes care of the *letter*, the music becomes a one-dimensional analysis and will obstinately refuse to take wing. Before the first orchestral rehearsal, therefore, a conductor naturally studies the score to decide on how to interpret it; if familiar, to read it as if for the first time and if new, as if an old friend. Hermann Scherchen maintained that the conductor *'must hear the score as perfectly as the creator heard it. To conduct means to make manifest without flaws that which one has perfectly heard within oneself! Hearing inwardly what one sees on the page is the fundamental requisite for every kind of musical study. Failing it, music, instead of being the most human of all art practices, is merely the possibility of manipulating an instrument.'* Likewise Bruno Walter on Mahler wrote, *'He approached the score like a lover constantly wooing, always ready to re-consider, to improve and plumb new depths. Precision was a means to an end to bring the soul of the music to life. Only when his fiery hold over the singers and orchestra had established an absolute clarity of interpretation did he permit himself the free flight of spirit, which gave the performance the effect of improvisation. He believed that the best of music is not set down in the notes.'*

Before agreeing to conduct a particular work, a conductor has to be in sympathy with its 'meaning' or turn down the invitation. This was brought home to me early on when I conducted a work in which I didn't believe and as a result, felt decidedly uncomfortable from the very first rehearsal. On another occasion, whilst assisting a German 'metro-gnome', I was informed unequivocally that Mozart's *Die Zauberflöte* was 'kitsch', which shocked me as both Mozart and Schikaneder deeply expressed the fundamental precepts of humanity. The lack of warmth in the conductor's performance only confirmed my belief that a conductor should never work on a score for which he or she has no regard!

The general conception that conductors are in touch with the Infinite and disinterested in more mundane matters is belied by the detailed precision needed when planning rehearsals. A careful estimation of the number of rehearsals and the amount of time needed for each individual work is based on its complexity and/or unfamiliarity yet should a conductor finish early for whatever reason, another rehearsal is rarely granted or a later one extended. Players have even been known to put down their instruments in the middle of a phrase as time was up, though it must be said that the vast majority are amenable to an extra few minutes without overtime if the conductor has their respect. Another consideration has to be those rehearsals when extra players such as a third or fourth percussionist or a contra-bassoonist are to be called for; it not only saves unnecessary expense for the management but also the gratitude of those players who can then accept other engagements.

Valuable time and energy is also saved for everyone when the conductor checks the full score against the orchestral parts, which is tedious; but erasing unwanted markings and gratuitous graffiti is a salutary reminder of what players have to suffer from badly faded print and tattered parts. Some have the bars numbered in fives and tens while the full score has rehearsal letters or neither, causing another frustration when searching for a suitable place to re-commence. Various editions of the same work can also have radical differences as with Rossini's *Barber of Seville* in which a flute phrase in the score materialises from the cellos, sometimes to the embarrassment of the conductor. This 'spring cleaning' is especially useful during the early stages of a career for it assists the memorisation process but an established conductor usually has an orchestral librarian to do what's necessary.

Facing the inevitable

The Principal Horn in the Munich orchestra (Richard's Strauss' father) summed up the first encounter of a conductor with an orchestra as *'when a man walks to the rostrum and opens his score, even before he picks up his baton, we know whether he is the master or we'*. Facing a new orchestra can be quite tense and it usually takes till after the break in the first rehearsal to relax, yet the conductor has to 'rehearse' him or herself <u>at the same time</u>. An internal running commentary by an *alter ego* might include whether to repeat an awkward passage or see if it is still a problem during a reprise of the passage at the next rehearsal? Was the mishap due to an ambiguous gesture or the player? Would a change of bow improve the phrasing and is there still sufficient time to begin a new movement? Bruno Walter wrote, *'Never allow your feelings to over-ride completely your spirit of observation and sense of control'*, while the less gracious Celibidache stated, *'A rehearsal isn't music. A rehearsal means you say NO constantly. Not so fast, not so loud, not so dull, no, no, no, how many times, and "yes" only once.'* The difficulty is to find a balance between *feelings* and *control*, though conductors sometimes forget that players are as naked as they themselves while players forget that conductors are only human and yet have to cope with pressures way beyond their own. Rehearsal psychology is therefore very important and, as Mariss Janssons noted, *'You have to arrive knowing what you want in terms of sound and interpretation, but I try not to explain too much. If musicians are intelligent, you should not lecture them, you should just say a little about balance and dynamics. Of course all this depends on their technique, but the most important thing is their spiritual understanding. Your eyes and hands have to communicate through energy, not through being a musicologist. Music cannot be explained. It's about feelings, not brains. Physically it's not too hard to get a hundred people to play properly. The challenge is to set the spiritual tone and to unite them with one pulse. It makes the musicians connect with each other. How it happens is a complete mystery, a chemical secret.'*

Rehearsal conditions vary from one country to another. Some orchestras rehearse for three hours including a fifteen-minute break while others for two hours and a half, and yet have the same fifteen-minute break. In one European country I found that the players took out a pack of cards and drank cognac during their twenty-minute break — a far cry from Mahler's four-hour rehearsals without any break. Reaction to the conductor's beat also varies, with European orchestras tending to play behind which is nerve-wracking for a novice conductor. American orchestras, on the other hand, have traditionally played exactly on the 'click' of the beat, producing thereby a sharper rhythmic bite.

Then there are non-musical problems that beset most orchestras such as seating configuration, the shape and comfort of their chairs, music stands, central heating, the lighting and the perennial problem of air-conditioning. The conductor's own needs are equally important, for the rostrum's size, width and height must allow for a comfortable stance and good posture. If too high, too low, too wide, too narrow, or without a guardrail, the conductor's physical and mental balance can be disturbed, especially for those who suffer from vertigo or indulge in balletics. Paradoxically the rostrum is not always the best place from which to hear: the woodwind may sound distant even though the sound penetrates over the conductor's head to the back of the auditorium: the harp's lowest register can be lost and the back desks of the strings not heard at all. In some configurations, the horns are seated to the left of the woodwind to allow for the sound to issue from their backward-facing bells to resonate off the walls. In others, they sit on the opposite side or next to the brass, but behind the woodwind their effect tends to be diminished while the timpani and percussion are raised above the other instruments, quite illogically considering that they are deafening at times.

Until approximately the middle years of the twentieth century, the 2nd Violins always sat to the right of the rostrum, so that the antiphonal writing in the upper strings favoured by earlier composers was clearly differentiated. Then with the advent of larger orchestras, bigger concert halls and greater complexity in string writing the seating plan was changed so that the 1st and 2nd Violins sat together to allow for better ensemble. Sir Adrian Boult never wavered from the older 'Continental' configuration affirming that *'placing them all together puts all the treble to the left and the entire base to the right, giving the audience a most unbalanced picture of the sound. The argument that the 1st and 2nd violins often play in octaves and unisons, bow together and therefore should sit together, is to me unim-*

portant. If the leader of the 2nd violins is of any use, he will secure a perfect ensemble.' A few conductors still insist on the Continental style, but the perpetual to-ing and fro-ing for the sake of different conductors is very disturbing, especially for the 2nd Violins who have to continually adjust their style of playing. With the Continental seating, the violas, cellos, and basses were to the centre in front of the conductor facing the audience, enhancing their sonority; so; apart from an occasional ensemble difficulty with some more recent scores, the older layout still has great merit.

Some conductors lay down an interpretative blueprint without any fuss during the rehearsal and then 'improvise' on it during the performance while others rehearse with tremendous energy and adopt a calm magisterial exterior during the concert allowing the musicians to perform with the minimum of fuss. One conductor may be admired (even worshipped) by the orchestra, yet have little appeal for an audience while another may have a strong following with the public but command little respect from the musician, but all should heed the advice that Leopold Mozart gave to his son. *'You should do your best to keep the whole orchestra in good humour; flatter them and cultivate all round attachment to yourself by judicious praise! Everyone, even the worst viola player, may be deeply stirred by personal praise and becomes so much the more zealous and attentive, while a little courtesy of that kind costs you no more than a word or two . . . . I merely mention it because rehearsals afford few opportunities of the kind and so one is likely to forget it till the opera is staged, when one first really notices any want of cordiality and zeal in the members of the orchestra!'*

Close encounters

The most important colleague for any conductor is the leader – also known as concert-master or mistress – for he or she is the litmus paper of the orchestra's morale. This multi-skilled musician mediates should problems occur and can imperceptibly rescue the orchestra if the conductor's concentration happens to falter for a moment. The leader is also responsible for sorting out the many practical irritations that frequently occur within the orchestra such as seating positions in the string department, personality clashes between woodwind and brass players, auditioning, advising the management and countless other matters. If that wasn't enough, before rehearsals even begin the leader devotes much time and effort to bowing the string parts or editing previous ones to match the current conductor's interpretation.

The relationship between conductor and soloist is also vitally important as however familiar a concerto may be, a meeting before the first rehearsal can make a great difference in resolving any differences in interpretation they may have. Without such a meeting, a battle of wits is likely in front of the orchestra with considerable loss of face for either, or both, but if the soloist blatantly ignores the composer's printed indications it is the conductor's responsibility to keep the orchestra on an even keel. An extreme example of what can happen was when I was conducting a Mozart piano concerto, the pianist missed out a lot of the passage work in the first movement and then jumped from the opening solo to the cadenza in the second movement. In the last movement she ignored the printed repeats even though we had rehearsed with them so the concerto ended in total confusion! Needless to say, we were completely unnerved for the next work on the programme, Wagner's *Siegfried Idyll*. Some soloists have a reputation for changing their interpretation between rehearsal and performance without being aware of the fact, but the conductor's worst nightmare is when the soloist literally takes over the rehearsal and usurps the conductor's authority: fortunately, the greater the artist, the more co-operative the soloist.

Composers who attend rehearsals of their latest work have also to be handled with care. Some perpetually interrupt while others believe that their work is now well and truly over sit at the back of the auditorium and only come forward to offer a few succinct words of advice and thanks. On the other hand, it has been known for a conductor to forbid any interference or show any respect for an anxious and expectant composer and, on the odd occasion, to ignore the composer completely.

The relationship with a record producer is quite unique in that the conductor has an external doppelgänger rather than an internal alter ego who can make artistic suggestions and give constructive advice. The reason being that working in the artificial and dry atmosphere of a studio with so much starting and stopping, conductors can lose touch with their original intention and be surprised when the play back is objectively scrutinised in the control booth. On the other hand, an egocentric megalomaniac shuns any advice from an underling while others detest the whole conception of fossilising their performance for posterity.

Conductors, like virtually all-performing artists nowadays, need the collaboration of an agent or manager. The difference between them is that the former finds engagements pure and simple, while the latter has an all-round involvement in their artist's progress and development. This includes travel and accommodation as well as being aware of the many professional undercurrents that can be exploited; such work necessitates considerable promotional skill (and financial overheads). As only one conductor is ever needed for any one engagement, managers have to assure the other conductors on their books that they are being equally promoted, which requires a considerable amount of diplomacy. An exclusive contract is often world-wide, and usually involves reciprocal arrangements with foreign counterparts; a non-exclusive contract implies that the artist can accept engagements from another agent or manager.

Applause, the audience and other critics

The sound of applause is extraordinary, being that it is an unmusical sound. But at the same time it is a measure of the artist's success both with the public and, consequently, with prospective employers. Some performances are applauded regardless of whether they have been good or bad, and in opera the orchestral conclusion of an aria is often drowned by vociferous applause. Similarly, in ballet the audience's applause of a dancer's entrance, solo and exit, virtually ignores the music. In the concert hall a tradition exists not to applaud between movements but this was not always the case and in the eighteenth and early nineteenth centuries, entirely different music (and even by a different composer) was inserted between movements. Hissing and booing occurs quite regularly in Germany and Italy and more recently elsewhere, and some countries have a tradition of showing their approval with a slow rhythmic handclap though in other countries it has derisive connotations.

When Fred Blanks, the music critic of the *Sydney Morning Herald*, retired in July 1996, he reflected on the critic's role, which makes interesting reading for those who fail to appreciate or prefer not to understand their function. '*Criticism of the arts is not an international conspiracy against creativity, but, when practised with integrity, it is a constructive promotion of understanding between the creator of art and its beholder. A music critic must love music. A critic asks himself whom he is addressing. He is not an agent for composers, performers or promoters, though they all find him useful when he plays their tune. He is primarily responsible to his medium and readers . . . Unfortunately, the media — no exceptions — are replacing such critical assessment with the kind of pre-digested commercial puffery which advertisers cherish. The reasons are, of course, financial . . . Critics strike a fine balance between objectivity and subjectivity.*'

Performers are flattered by a complimentary review even when strongly denied and shun the opposite without question, but if they accept the former as just, then the latter must be equally so. What may appear to be scathing at first sometimes becomes innocuous, even complimentary with the passing of time, and a bad review is better read on the supposition that it contains a grain of truth and a rave review read with scepticism as all criticism like performing is subjective. A damning review can be especially daunting for a conductor who has to face the orchestra at the next rehearsal knowing full well that the players might have read it. The materialistic value of a review is as a visiting card for an agent or manager to explore professional openings for their clients but General Managers of orchestras and opera companies are likely to quote a complimentary one and ignore a bad one when expediency demands! There is an unwritten law in the profession that one should never reply to a critic as the pen is mightier than the baton.

Metro-gnome: Conductor, Maestro

The title Maestro (Italian for Master) is accepted to mean a highly respected conductor but it is often used incorrectly for any conductor, whether good or bad (but a metro-gnome can be easily spotted). What distinguishes the real Maestro from the Conductor is far more difficult and only fully understood perhaps by observation of one in action although Debussy – when writing as Monsieur Croce, antidilettante – came near to doing so. *'If Hans Richter looks like a prophet, when he conducts the orchestra he is the Almighty, and you may be sure that God himself would have asked him for some hints before embarking on such an adventure.'* Arguably, the illusive difference is that of an innate degree of talent bordering on genius but Sergiu Celibidache, a Maestro of more recent times, expressed his philosophy in a television interview as: *'there is no definition of music. It exists outside thought. Whatever is created, is outside thought but it must be put together by means of thought . . . There is a relation between what I hear and the inner world of my feelings. This relationship makes music possible . . . All you can do is let it happen. You don't do anything yourself but you make sure that nothing happens which could in any way impede the wonderful process. So, you are incredibly active, and at the same time, incredibly passive. You don't want anything; you just let it happen . . . Each concert hall, each piece of music, each movement has its own tempo which reflects its unique situation. Understanding it is just the beginning. Even when you understand, you are not inside it yet. What matters are experiencing it . . . Tradition is a vague concept of what others have done. A piece of music, like tradition, doesn't exist but is born anew each and every time. Those relying on tradition are impotent.'*

If only batons were engraved with *'Was ist denn Musik? Musik ist eine heilige Kunst'* (*What then is music? Music is a noble art'*, Ariadne auf Naxos, Hofmannsthal/Strauss) for, along with Stanford's tinkling bell at the tip, it might help to keep a conductor's necessary egotistical megalomania balanced by humility, a point that is well illustrated by an apocryphal story concerning Toscanini and Piatigorsky. Just before going on stage to perform a concerto, Toscanini rounded on Piatigorsky for being the worst cellist in the world, lacking rhythm, phrasing, sensitivity and virtually every other quality needed to be a good musician. Piatigorsky was reduced to a quivering jelly but Toscanini then proceeded to demolish himself for being hopeless at controlling an orchestra, lacking a stick technique and having a deficient ear. But continued, *'However, there's no one better than us, is there.'* Another legend has it that one particular Maestro would concentrate on a geranium in a pot before a concert and when it began to wilt, he knew he was ready to walk out to the rostrum. Another, who suffered badly from nerves, would try to lock himself in the toilet but was always thwarted by an attendant who got in first so that there was no alternative but to go out to face the music. But having walked through the orchestra and reached the podium virtually all conductors emanate an aura of calm command (like a ship's captain) to both the orchestra and the audience even though it may be a façade, while underneath may lie doubts of one sort or another. As the performance has to be a re-creation of the composer's spirit and not merely a reading of the letter (the notes) an honest conductor is never totally satisfied but has to continually strive to do better despite any ecstatic applause by the audience. Elgar knew this when he headed his *Second Symphony* with the opening lines of a poem by Shelley, *'Rarely, rarely comest thou spirit of delight!'*

In the Theatre

The operatic microcosm

'Opera is an exotic and irrational entertainment which has always been combated, and always prevailed.' Dr. Johnson was referring to his compatriots who preferred their opera sung in Italian rather than English but opera today involves at least three major foreign languages – and a few others for good measure – as well as any number of exotic and irrational situations.

The General Manager

It might be imagined that the Music Director has the ultimate authority in an opera company but that is seldom the case. More often than not it is the General Manager, who may prefer the alternative titles of General Administrator, General Director or Intendant as in Germany. Some General Managers fulfil both functions of G.M. and Artistic Director, and dispense with the services of a Music Director. Whatever the title, the position is highly complex and stressful for opera is a labour intensive 'industry' in which crises of one sort or another occur on a day to day basis. Rudolf Bing, Glyndebourne's first General Manager, who later held the same position at the Metropolitan Opera, New York, said that underneath his hard exterior there lay a heart of stone. His successor in Sussex, Moran Caplat, espoused a similar philosophy: it was essential to have principles, but be prepared to ignore them when necessary!

The Music Director

The Music Director is under the General Manager. Being more in the public arena than the General Manager, this situation can lead to strife, nevertheless there have been many great collaborations despite well-publicised fracas. Should differences arise, the Music Director is often the loser for the simple reason that the General Manager usually sits on the Board while the conductor doesn't unless of course his or her ambition for power is equally strong. The Music Director's responsibilities include choosing a balanced repertoire and casting (in consultation with the G.M. of course), the selection of guest and staff conductors, the appointment of a Chorus Master and the artistic direction of the orchestra. The Music Director also appoints a Head of Music Staff who, in turn, auditions repetiteurs, prompters, language coaches and new talent, and is ultimately responsible for the day to day musical aspects of the company. Now that Music Directors accept many more guest appearances elsewhere than previously, the Head of Music Staff has become even more vital, especially if a Music Director has been appointed with little prior knowledge of opera, not having served an apprenticeship as a repetiteur. As a result of inexperience they are unaware that singers have a different mental approach to instrumentalists and that opera is not only music but also that the dramatic element has to be taken into consideration. The drama inherent in the music therefore demands more than usual changes of tempo, flexibility of the recitatives punctuated by chords, orchestral silence for many bars, the holding of pauses, waiting for the set to be changed and countless other theatrical matters. In fact, the timing of the drama is literally in the hands of the conductor who is not in the pit to be merely a reliable accompanist as the opera-going public sometimes imagine. On occasion a conductor may have to save a performance from catastrophe because a singer has a memory lapse, requiring the jump of a bar or two, which can be disastrous if the orchestra isn't fully alert and unsure whether to follow the singer or the conductor. Even the set may create problems as, when during *Madama Butterfly*, Susuki's house fell in on itself like a pack of cards because the stage crew had forgotten to secure the scenery.

The singer

Singers are different from instrumentalists in that their vocal chords are internal whereas a violin, clarinet or any other instrument is visible to its executant. Singers may also discover that they have a vocal talent only at the time of puberty or just after, having missed out on training in musicianship, which, it must be stated, is not necessarily the same as having musicality. Because the voice is internal, its tuition and development largely depends on the digestion of pictorial and dramatic images physiologically conveyed to the vocal chords, which then react instinctively. Understandably, singers' paramount concern is health as even the slightest cold can affect their livelihood. Singers working in opera also have quite a number of extra tasks, over and above producing a good voice and knowing the music. They have to memorise extensive roles, comprehend every nuance and inflection in more than one foreign language, remember the production, follow a conductor despite being blinded by powerful lights and change costume a number of times during a performance. *'The old maestri teach the young singers, and the old singers teach the young maestri'* used to be an oft-heard refrain but it now seems to have been forgotten, more is the pity.

Opera production

Opera being the ultimate fusion of music, text and drama, it is necessary to involve two artistic directors unlike the straight theatre in which actors only require one. Compatibility is therefore essential between the conductor and the producer for, when clashes occur, the unfortunate singers are caught in the middle, confused by contradictory demands. So, in order to fuse music and production, the music has first to be digested, as the two entities cannot be absorbed at the same time. The singers are initially coached by repetiteurs and when the conductor arrives they are then moulded into an ensemble ready for the production rehearsals to begin. For a new production the ensemble rehearsals, especially for the Mozart operas with their complex ensembles and multi-layered characters, have a considerable number of calls but a revival usually requires fewer as the cast is already conversant with the opera and any corrections can be made during the production period.

Production rehearsals extend to two or three weeks depending on the complexity of the opera, during which a circumspect conductor adopts a subordinate position. But a conductor unaccustomed to working in opera find this "demotion" difficult to accept even though it is only temporary. Conversely the conductor who perpetually interrupts in order to correct mistakes because the singer is concentrating on the production may annoy the producer. One practical solution is for the conductor to take note of any such errors by using bookmarks, paper and a pencil which, incidentally, can also be used in lieu of a baton. When the production has reached an advanced stage, the conductor departs to prepare the orchestra after which one, two and possibly three piano dress rehearsals take place on stage in the theatre to modify or correct any technical problems and/or to modify the sight lines. Despite the ever-present possibility of disagreement, when the conductor and producer are aware of each other's territory and willing to collaborate, the rehearsal period can become an exhilarating experience for all concerned.

During the *sitzprobe* (seated rehearsal) the singers concentrate on listening to, and singing with, the orchestra as previously the rehearsals were with a piano and the orchestral sound has a totally different colour and resonance. The rehearsal can be tense as the singers are conscious of being judged by their peers in the orchestra while the conductor has the problem of playing the entire opera in three hours with little time to repeat a difficult passage that has not quite gelled. During the orchestra with stage rehearsals the conductor then weds the singers — now concentrating equally on the production and the music — with the orchestra while the producer has to accept the inevitable situation that the conductor is in command once more. By the Dress Rehearsal (General Rehearsal) — sometimes open to an invited audience — the opera has become a total entity and ready for the paying public.

The baton in the pit

Dance has always been intrinsic to music, with the highly structured court dances and Masques of the aristocracy superseded by such classical dances as the Minuet followed by the folk dances and waltzes of Central Europe. Like their operatic colleagues, ballet conductors often launch their careers as repetiteurs with dance companies but whereas a conductor can hold a pause for a singer's high note, once a dancer is in the air, the law of gravity comes into operation. That is not to decry the skill of conducting for ballet as there have been a number of conductors with an innate feeling for dancers yet still able to conduct the intrinsic shape of the music without any distortion of the composer's intentions. I myself took part in Movement classes and as an impoverished student in London regularly extemporised polkas, waltzes, minuets etc. for ballet classes, and later conducted for television, a ballet choreographed by Leonide Massine the great dancer.

Opera pits now come in all shapes and sizes but the first opera houses were without any as there was good visual and audible contact between singers, players and conductor and balance and co-ordination problems were minimal. With the building of the larger opera houses, orchestra pits had to be built to house the expanding orchestras which in turn led to the singers having to project their voices into larger theatres which gave rise to the technique known as *bel canto*. Contact between conductor, and singer has always been something of a problem with so many people on stage (and occasionally animals) but nowadays the majority of opera houses are equipped with amplifiers and closed circuit television. Although it has made contact much easier, the monitors have created a problem for the conductor who yearns for direct personal contact with the singer and another for an irascible Diva having six or seven conductor-clones all gesticulating at her from a myriad of monitors in perfect ensemble!

Physical stamina is vitally necessary when conducting an opera as a performance may take up to four hours or more whereas a concert is usually much shorter and made up of music by as many as four or five composers each with a distinctive style. The conductor of a concert, therefore, has to switch from one style to another very quickly while an opera has only one. Likewise, any one concert may be repeated two or three times at most, but an opera has many performances in any one season and it is a challenge to maintain a consistently high performance level at every performance. Berlioz exploited this fact of orchestral life in his book *Les Soirées de l'orchestre*, which consisted of twenty-five evenings and two epilogues. One story differentiated between types of applause, another the life cycle of a tenor, and a third described Euphonia the capital of Concordia, a utopian country in which the population spent their lives entirely devoted to music. The shortest stories were those when the players were busy concentrating on a masterpiece by a favourite composer. One ended with the conductor being so overcome that he chewed his baton to pulp, shook every player's hand in utter silence as he stepped down from the rostrum, and disappeared in a cloud of perspiration.

Janus on the Podium

Metamorphosis

The forerunner of the modern conductor was the cantor who led the chanting of plainsong in the cathedrals and monasteries of Europe. Then, as music evolved to become a secular entertainment, the instrumental ensembles had to be co-ordinated by the principal violinist or the continuo player, usually the composer. Conducting was still basically a wave of the bow or a nod of the head that musicians took as their cue to begin; only an occasional gesture was necessary. Jazz music today is similar in that the bandleader indicates the tempo with a basic indication of 1,2,3,4, and thereafter there is no real need for a conductor as the beat remains constant. This was also the practice until the baroque era drew to a close when, as orchestras increased in size, the stringed instruments filled out the inner harmonic structure, making the continuo player redundant. It was then but a short step for the principal violinist to move to the more visible central position and the art of conducting, as we know it today, began to emerge.

Beethoven was among the first to conduct from the central position *'without a regular or continuous beat'* as one commentator noted, which so infuriated the orchestra that they banned him from rehearsals and he had to write down his intentions which were then passed to the orchestra from another room. We tend to assume that the orchestra in Vienna was somewhat comparable to one of today but at that time (1807) it consisted of 55 players of whom only 18 were professionals and the remaining 37 (twice as many) were amateur. Beethoven's friend, Anton Schindler, wrote about the time of the première of his *First Symphony* that the orchestras was *'certainly not lacking in brave fellows but lacking rather in good will, team spirit and love of art, thus the ensemble is rather poor'*. A few years later his opinion was still virtually the same: *'They are insufficiently and poorly rehearsed . . . If a composer was able to get them to play the right notes in one or, at the most, two rehearsals, he had to be satisfied with the results. As for any notion whatsoever of deeper nuances, Viennese orchestras lack both the capacity and interest!'* For the first ever performance of Beethoven's *Ninth (Choral) Symphony* in 1824, there were only two rehearsals so it must have been chaotic even allowing for the composer's deafness and eccentric gestures of crouching when he wanted them to play softly and jumping for the loud passages! Not long afterwards the young Richard Wagner noted that for a performance of the same symphony in Leipzig, the instrumental movements were still directed by the principal violinist and a 'time beater' only came on stage to conduct the choral finale. It took another fifteen years before he could fully appreciate the work when in Paris he attended a performance conducted by Habeneck. *'The scales fell from my eyes. I came to understand the value of correct execution and the secret of good performance. The orchestra had learned to look for Beethoven's melody in every bar and the orchestra SANG the melody. That was the secret. Habaneck was not a conductor of special genius but he persisted until every member of the orchestra understood the music. He was the master and they obeyed him . . . The orchestra sang the symphony and therefore the true tempo had been found.'*

The art and craft of conducting was developing, though Berlioz in his *Grand traité d'instrumentation et d'orchestration modernes* (Treatise on modern instrumentation and orchestration) was quite scathing about some of its practitioners. *'Conductors are more dangerous than singers, as bad singers only damage their own parts; the incapable or malevolent conductor ruins everything . . . He should know the composition he conducts, the nature of the instruments and he should know how to read a score. Above all, the most indefinable talent for transmitting his feelings to the orchestra. If this is denied him, then power and authority completely escapes him, he is no longer a chief, a director, but a mere wielder of the baton, a simple beater of time even supposing he knows how to beat and divide the time properly.'* Berlioz stressed the need 'to know and read a score' yet Habaneck, who Wagner had praised for his performance of the *Choral Symphony*, still conducted the work from the 1st Violin part.

Liszt was equally pungent in his comments about the art and

craft. *'As there has been an advance in the execution of rhythm, the manner of phrasing and the bringing out of the light and shade of music, I have tried to establish with the players a different kind of bond from that which is cemented by the imperturbable beating of time. For the works of Beethoven, Berlioz and Wagner, etc. I see fewer advantages than elsewhere (and even elsewhere would contest them) in the conductor functioning like a windmill, sweating profusely, the better to communicate warmth to his personnel. In these works above all, where it is a question of understanding and feeling, a question of addressing the intelligence and of firing hearts in communion with the beautiful, the great and true in art and poetry, the capacity and ancient routine of the average maitre de chapel are no longer adequate, indeed are contrary to the dignity and sublime freedom of art. The real task of the conductor consists in my opinion in making himself ostensibly quasi-useless. We are pilots, not drillmasters.'*

The charismatic conductor had now arrived on the scene in the form of Wagner whose style was described by Felix Weingartner, a formidable conductor of a later generation, as *'He was bent on bringing out that which the sounds and notes are only a means to an end. He sought the unifying thread, the psychological line, the revelation of which suddenly transforms, as if by magic a more or less indefinite picture into a beautifully shaped heart-moving vision . . . He had a body of no more than middle height, with a stiff deportment, the movement of the arms not immoderately great or sweeping, but decisive and very much to the point. He showed no restlessness in spite of his vivacity and usually did not need a score at the concert. He would fix his expressive glance on the players, ruling them imperiously. The players had no sense of being led. Each believed himself to be following freely his own feeling, yet they all worked together wonderfully.'*

Wagner's towering personality had a tremendous influence on both the conductors who worked as his assistants and on the audiences who were conditioned to accept his Music Dramas as 'High Art' and expected to worship at the feet of its protagonists, the conductors. The era of the autocrat of the rostrum was now well and truly established with most of them appointed by Boards of Direction made up of philanthropists, impresarios, society hostesses, and patrons of the arts who seldom showed an interest in the welfare of the players. Orchestral musicians were not yet employed on a permanent basis and could be hired and fired at will, but as the Musicians Union began to gain a foothold, working conditions improved and some players even had an input into their board's policy making. By the 1940s, and perhaps as a result of Sir Thomas Beecham and the London Philharmonic Orchestra parting company, a player was appointed as the orchestra's General Manager which heralded the wane of the autocratic conductor who, instead, had to collaborate with the players as respected equals rather than as underlings. Richard Adeney, the principal flautist in one of the London orchestras at that time, observed this new situation as: *'Conductors don't have the power now to sack or intimidate. With our self-governing orchestras, if a man is really unpleasant, and unmusical into the bargain, we kick him out straightway.'*

At the crossroads

Orchestras are also becoming flexible though there is a danger that in endeavouring to attract a new audience, some advertise on the commercial bandwagon and it is by no means certain that those who are lured in this way go on to explore 'classical' music further. *Amadeus*, the highly successful film at the box office, would have supposedly attracted a new audience and similarly free concerts or those entirely devoted to 'top of the pops' classical music haven't made much of a difference. One (reputable) music magazine has suggested using strobe lighting and electronic amplification as used by pop groups and it is not beyond the realms of possibility that concert-halls may soon have video screens with the conductors projected on them larger than life (if that were possible). Conductors may then perhaps be expected to wear advertisements on their backs like athletes or racing-car drivers so that Sir Adrian Boult's desire that conductors be heard and <u>not</u> seen will be abandoned forever. This is not to deny that some musicians have allowed themselves to be exploited for their commercial potential. Joachim, for instance lent his name to *'Steinway is to the pianist what*

Stradivarius is to the violinist' and Wagner, similarly *'A Beethoven Sonata, a Bach Chromatic Fantasie, can only be fully appreciated when rendered upon one of your Pianofortes'*, so it's really a matter of degree and fashion or taste. Promoting a recording may now take the form of a sexy female violinist on the sleeve for Brahms or a helicopter gunship for *Die Götterdämmerung*. Snippets of Bach and Vivaldi help to improve sales for toilet paper, Wagner and Holst do the same for cars, and Mozart sells anything. Opera companies have gone down the same path and have little compunction about lacing their brochures with subliminal exhortations that subscribers will enjoy the performance even before setting foot in the theatre!

The quasi religious High Art as espoused by Wagner has virtually gone the way of all flesh and 'classical' music has joined the realms of Entertainment and is sold using the same advertising techniques as pop, rap, jazz, rock, folk, country and western, world music (whatever that means) and video games. The only difference is that whereas a piece of pop music lasts for approximately ten minutes, even a relatively short symphony is considerably longer and demands greater concentration and commitment. While supposedly immersed in a recording of a Mahler symphony it is now possible to fast-forward, scan the newspaper, order a pizza, transmit a fax, chat on a mobile, and surf the Internet. This incredible technology combined with the cost of running orchestras and the expense now involved in going to concerts and opera has already had an effect outside the major centres of music in the Western world with many second and third tier orchestras closing down. Orchestras, and consequently conductors, are increasingly at the mercy of accountants, who having little interest in the intangible spiritual value of music epitomised in (hopefully) a tongue in cheek audit report from an anonymous source. *'For considerable periods the four oboe players have nothing to do so their numbers should be reduced and the work spread more evenly over the whole of the concert thus eliminating peaks of activity. All the twelve first violins were playing identical notes which seems an unnecessary duplication and the staff of this section should be drastically cut. If a large* volume of sound is required, it could be obtained by electronic amplification. Much effort was absorbed in the playing of semi-quavers which seems an excessive refinement so it's recommended that all notes should be rounded up to the nearest quaver. If this were done it would be possible to use trainees and lower grade operatives more extensively. There seems to be too much repetition of some musical passages. No useful purpose is served by repeating on the horns a passage which has already been played by the strings. Scores could therefore be drastically pruned and the whole time of two hours could be reduced to twenty minutes which would also reduce the need for an intermission. The conductor agrees generally with these recommendations but expressed the opinion that there might be some falling off in attendance. In that unlikely event it should be possible to close sections of the auditorium entirely with a consequent saving in overhead expenses such as lighting and salaries of ushers etc.'

While the above is an amusing exaggeration, it is based on a grain of truth as confirmed recently by an eminent Australian musician. *'I have been going to concerts for 40 years and there is absolutely no doubt in my mind that concert programming has become markedly more conservative, and that is due to marketing factors. Marketing managers run the performing arts system. I've sat at meetings where marketing managers have vetoed concerts. This is a problem because very often, marketing people have little idea of what they are marketing, with the result that they undersell or miss opportunities for marketing their own product. Everything has to be dumbed down and sugarcoated!'* The current situation may affect the future not only of conductors but classical music in general but there are signs that many orchestras and opera companies are aware of the problem so the future need not necessarily be as bleak as it appears to be. Following the model of Leonard Bernstein and his dynamic wooing of young audiences, there are now many projects to do just that. Orchestras and opera companies are inspiring future generations with much more of a 'hands on' approach than was practised by music educators in the past. They now capture the imagination at an early age, allowing even the very young to explore the instruments in the orchestra in a practical way, and similar projects are under way in opera where young people are actively involved in much of what happens back stage as well as on stage. When young people are exposed in this 'user friendly way' to the ogre of classical music there is no doubt that they are stirred by it, which lays the foundation for both future adult audiences and performers alike. But these exciting developments haven't as yet reached their full potential as described by Berlioz in his *Les Soirèes de l'orchestre*. In his utopian city of Euphonia, the entire population sang in choirs or played in orchestras, they made instruments and took pride in producing beautifully printed scores. Euphonia's thoroughfares had names like Harp Avenue, Tuba Boulevard and Piccolo Alley and such like, and education included not only vocal and instrumental tuition but also harmony, counterpoint and rhythm, so that by puberty, the young adults were able to fully appreciate and enjoy art and beauty. Berlioz set his Euphonia in the year 2344 so by then, a conductor arriving by space craft will discover that the current developments in music education will (hopefully) have borne fruit.

A Personal Pilgrim's Progress

There are no assured paths to the rostrum though I have observed that determination, resilience in adversity, and good fortune are equally important as is an innate ability, and that it's often an unexpected decision that develops into something more important than was first imagined. This section outlines my own experience as an example of just one of the ways by which a conducting career may unfold.

The wand of youth

My *Gradus ad Parnassum* began in Devon when I began to have lessons with Dr. John Wray – my first mentor who later became the Registrar of the Royal Manchester College of Music. He not only taught me the basics of piano playing but also score reading, harmony, figured bass, the five species of 'strict' counterpoint, and basic orchestration. I quickly dismissed the idea of becoming a concert pianist as it was too much like hard work for, as John once said, *'I had a lot in common with Artur Rubinstein, neither of us practised'*. I subsequently decided to become a composer but my attempts were regurgitated Debussy and Vaughan-Williams, and after sitting for hours by the river Dart to soak up the atmosphere for a symphonic poem no inspiration ever descended. So there was only one path left for me to follow: conducting.

John's vast collection of records and scores and the BBC Northern and Scottish Orchestras opened up a Pandora's box and I can still recall the physical sensation of hearing *L'après-midi d'une faune* for the very first time, conducted by Beecham on an old wax record. Being completely ignorant of what conducting might actually entail and having never seen a conductor in action I conducted the radio with a knitting needle and for quite some time my 'baton' went to the right instead of the left, which later had to be painstakingly corrected.

At sixteen I became the conductor of the Torbay Male Voice Choir made up of men old enough to be my father (in some cases, my grandfather) and I had my first success by winning first prize at the local Competitive Festival with a choral arrangement of Lully's *Bois Epais*. I had viola lessons and taught myself the double bass well enough to scrape my way through Handel's *Messiah* and Gilbert & Sullivan. During the intense cold winter of 1947/48, an opera company came to Torquay with *La Bohème*, my first encounter with the 'exotic and irrational world of opera'. When the tenor started to sing *'Your tiny hand is frozen let me warm it next to mine'* my father (who may have thought himself into the character of Mimi) called out *'and so are my blessed feet'*. The first concert I ever attended was in Plymouth when Sir Adrian Boult conducted Beethoven and Borodin's *Second Symphony*. I was bowled over. At the time I never dreamt that I would have a conducting lesson from him many years later.

As my Grammar School days were drawing to a close I auditioned for the Arts College at Dartington where Imogen Holst was then the Director of Music. She was dressed in black from head to toe in a somewhat medieval style and looked into my eyes for what seemed like ages until she finally said, *'I think you will like it here'*. So ended my audition, but my country needed me for National Service (the Army), and by the time I was demobilised two years later Imogen had moved to Aldeburgh to work for Benjamin Britten. Years later when I was rehearsing the BBC Chorus for Imogen, when she conducted her father's opera *Savitri*, I sensed that she had forgotten me and I refrained from reminding her of that previous occasion. At the end of my two futile years in the army, and having been told that I would never make a soldier, my Discharge Document stated that my conduct was *'Very good. His work has been entirely satisfactory. He is a conscientious and reliable young man who does his best. He is interested in music and intends to make it his career. He should succeed.'*

There had been no opportunity for practical music making apart from attending concerts in London on the odd weekend during those two years so my audition for the Royal Academy of Music was a disaster. I was asked *'When did Beethoven first use trombones?'* and I replied *'in the Eroica Symphony'*, which was wrong and consequently I failed the audition. However, having already been accepted by Dartington, I gravitated there where John Clements – one time the BBC's Chorus Master – had been appointed after Imogen's departure. In my two years at Dartington I learnt a great deal about choral training by observing every gesture he made while singing in his choir, as there was no conductor training course as such. Joan Cross and Anne Wood came with their recently opened Opera School to perform Mozart's *Bastien and Bastienne* and Ethyl Smythe's *The Boatswain's Mate*, and John entrusted me with training our few male students for the chorus' pub-crawl scene in the latter opera. Practically the first thing that Joan Cross asked me was, *'Do you play the piano accordion'* to which I replied *'No'*. *'Well you had better go away and learn it then, hadn't you'* was her imperious command. Joan was a formidable lady fashioned from the same mould as Edith Sitwell, Edith Evans and Margaret Rutherford. She was the personification of Lady Billows in *Albert Herring* who, in fact, Britten had modelled on her: Joan, like Lady Billows, even had a housekeeper called Florence! Naturally I did as she had commanded and managed to teach myself the piano accordion, later making my stage debut both as an accordion player and as a chorister. She presented me with a vocal score of *Così fan tutte* inscribed by her in the fly leaf, and after Joan and Anne persuaded Eileen Joyce (the famous Australian concert pianist) to sponsor a scholarship for repetiteurs, of which I was the first recipient.

Cockaigne calling

The Opera School at that time was housed in the De Walden Institute in St. John's Wood where I studied much of the standard repertoire with Vilem Tausky and sat in on Peter Gellhorn's coaching sessions with the student singers. My piano technique left much to be desired so I worked hard with Peter and he took me through Bach's fifteen three-part Inventions to develop both my hands to create three cantabile (singing) melodies without resorting to the sustaining pedal. Peter had a stock of proverbs of which one was a particular favourite with him, *'God is unkind. We are all granted 95% of what is required but it's up to us to discover the remaining 5% for ourselves.'* I conducted for Joan's production classes and was able to see what effect my conducting was having on both the music and the singers; as my 'orchestra' was a pianist, I could make mistakes in relative privacy. Joan could be quite crushing, as when she informed me that Benjamin Britten was writing a new opera for children called *Noyes Fludde* and I asked if it was like *Lets make an Opera*: her haughty reply was, *'Mr. Britten never repeats himself'*. Her female students would sometimes break down in tears and she would simply respond with *'It's better to learn now how demanding our profession can be rather than later.'* One particularly pithy comment was that we had to use our elbows to make any sort of career: a fact of professional life that I was to witness many times yet I myself failed to observe.

During the Second World War Joan had managed Sadlers Wells single handed and over-ruled the company's objection to performing a new work by a relatively unknown composer: *Peter Grimes* by Benjamin Britten. It was a spectacular success and turned out to be a turning point for opera in England with Joan herself as Ellen Orford. She created the roles of Female Chorus in *The Rape of Lucretia*, Lady Billows in *Albert Herring*, Queen Elizabeth I in *Gloriana* and Mrs. Gross in *The Turn of the Screw*, and when it was revived Joan asked me to play the score for her while she re-studied the part. Joan produced *Albert Herring* with the students in the Opera School which we took to Dartington, but one by one the cast was decimated by a flu epidemic until, as a last resort, Joan herself went on as Lady Billows. A number of years had passed since her previous performance in the role so she wrote some of the cue words in the palm of her hand and, not having had a rehearsal with her, I took her first act aria a shade too fast. Instantaneously an electric spark shot from her and my baton responded like a lightning conductor.

My first professional conducting engagement was in Eire with Verdi's *Rigoletto* and Flotow's *Martha*. It was an excellent way of discovering how to improve the playing of a less than good orchestra and, at the same time, practice using minimal body movement or I would have fallen into the mud that lay in the orchestra pit. In London I failed auditions for both Sadlers Wells and Covent Garden but I began to earn a living as a music copyist, as from studying many orchestral scores I had developed speed and accuracy and was able hear complete phrases in my head. A little known composer, Robert Still, asked me to copy his music, which in due course led to recording a choral work of his for Decca and to conduct his *Third Symphony* at the Royal Festival Hall followed by a recording of the same work for the Lyrita Record Edition. As a result, Lyrita asked me to record the first two symphonies of Arnold Bax with the London Philharmonic Orchestra – all having stemmed from my ability as a copyist.

Peter Gellhorn put forward my name to conduct a new musical. *The Comedy of Errors*, by Julian Slade the composer of *Salad Days*, which had been scored for an ensemble of flute, clarinet, percussion, cello and piano. The young cast included Patricia Routledge, more recently the redoubtable Hyacinth Bucket in *Keeping up Appearances*, and during our season she asked me for my opinion as to whether she had a possible career in opera. I could only answer, *'possibly with more vocal training'*, but as it happened her decision not to change direction turned out to be the better one. I also conducted for the Park Lane Opera Group the first English production of Bizet's *Le Docteur Miracle* coupled with Milhaud's *Le Pauvre Matelot*, a black comedy lasting only twenty minutes. Another venture was Group 8 which I and seven others formed as a 'shop window' for our various talents. At the St. Pancras (now Camden) Festival we gave the first performance in England of Rossini's *La Pietra del Paragone* and to my astonishment, the Italian Government awarded me a medal *Per Servizio della Musica e Cultura Italiana* for promoting Rossini's first ever opera. Our next Festival production was Phillis Tate's opera, *The Lodger* (Jack the Ripper) with Yvonne Minton – who had just arrived from Australia – making her London debut and with whom I was to work again on the première of Nicholas Maw's *One Man Show*. In one particular scene the Director of the National Gallery sings while standing on his head to examine the painting which is the subject of the opera. The tenor was Roger Norrington who has since become an esteemed international conductor and knighted.

There was still very little training of aspiring conductors and to rectify the situation Charles Groves (later knighted), the conductor of the Bournemouth Symphony Orchestra, ran a four-day course in 1957; from thirty-nine applicants twelve of us were chosen. One of his many pertinent comments that has stayed with me was that

'*Conducting is the art of a blind man, leading the lame, through a fog*': obviously an exaggeration and said to stir our thoughts but experience has shown it to be not that far from reality. It wasn't a conducting competition as such, but three of the twelve shared the conducting of the concluding concert though I was not among them. However, Arthur Jacobs writing in *The Sunday Times*, commented that '*a different judge might have preferred Myer Fredman*', which was certainly encouraging.

Sojurn in Sussex

The year 1959 saw two equally unimaginable events: a Russian unmanned spacecraft landing on the moon and I being accepted by Glyndebourne. Peter Gellhorn had recommended me to Jani Strasser and being invited to audition on January 1st seemed to be a good omen. He put a vocal score of *Così fan tutte* on the piano and opened it at the Act I Finale to see how I followed a conductor, the basic requirement for any repetiteur. I knew the opera well and was confident though naturally nervous and waited for him to start conducting: after a long silence he finally said: '*Well, why don't you begin?*' I did and quickly realised that he couldn't actually conduct but somehow conveyed what he wanted with both his hands and feet even if they weren't always in the same tempo! I left his house assuming that I had failed but later learnt that he had liked my conducting of *Dr. Miracle* at the Camden Festival and with Peter Gellhorn's recommendation for good measure accepted me. The Glyndebourne coaches included Geoffrey Parsons, Paul Hamburger and Martin Isepp but Jani needed a conductor for the back-stage orchestra in *Der Rosenkavalier* and to assist Peter with the chorus. I was to be engaged for six weeks to work on the rehearsals and performances of the Strauss and the chorus rehearsals of *Idomeneo* at the princely salary of £11 a week. When I modestly explained to the Assistant General Manager that the salary was actually less than the Musician's Union rate and we were expecting our first child, Douglas Craig replied that I would be learning far more from

Glyndebourne than it from me during my first season – and, I assumed my last – but he would see what he could do. When the letter arrived there was no mention of an increase but of course I signed the contract rather than lose the fantastic opportunity of working in one of the most prestigious opera houses in the world. When Douglas became General Manager of the Welsh National Opera he invited me to conduct *La traviata* and later still our paths were to cross again, and this time it was my turn to engage him. Douglas produced *Pelléas et Mélisande* with my Opera School students in Sydney which was something I would never have believed possible in 1959!

When I arrived in Sussex a secretary showed me around and misread my name so from that moment on I was known as Friar Madman though Erna Gal (Hernia Gallbladder) always called me by the Austrian diminutive, Myerlein. My first duty was to conduct the chorus under the stage soon after the start of Act II in *Der Rosenkavalier*. But one evening I didn't hear the warning bells at the end of the Interval, and arrived just as the chorus was finishing; fortunately Peter was there that night though I was sure my career was over before it had hardly begun. My other responsibility was conducting the back-stage café orchestra at the beginning of Act III, which has to be dovetailed with the main orchestra in the pit (sometimes in a different time signature) and is difficult co-ordinate. At the same time Octavian in the person of Elisabeth Söderström would be making her entrances and exits. When she was off-stage Elizabeth stood behind me and put her arms under mine and conducted along with me. It was particularly nerve-racking as I was trying to keep in time with Leopold Ludwig in the pit. In my letters home to my wife, Jeanne, I wrote that Jani must have surely realised how inept I was but I was wrong for I was engaged for the whole of the following year.

Jani could be madly infuriating and on one occasion a graphologist analysed his indecipherable handwriting and found him to be an egocentric megalomaniac so he must have been a conductor after all!

In the years that followed Jani was to be a great influence on me as on many others and he still crops up in conversation whenever colleagues meet today long after his death, which would have delighted him for he could never tolerate being ignored. His loyalty to Glyndebourne's standards was exemplary and he frequently reminded the music staff – and every one else for that matter – that over the Glyndebourne archway was inscribed (invisibly) the words *'the impossible is just a little harder to achieve'*. He was so determined to achieve the impossible that we were delegated to take notes on every performance and even on the last night of the season in readiness for the following one, even though the cast might be quite different! Every night and often till quite late after rehearsing and performing, I or another member of the music staff had to sit with him while he evolved the rehearsal schedule for the next day for all four or five operas, including costume and wig fittings. We suspected that he really needed us not to help but for company but I nevertheless learned to be meticulous when drawing up a rehearsal schedule. He dominated everyone, but at the same time disarmed us all with his unique sense of humour and fun. This is well reflected in the photo of Franco Zeffirelli strangling him in mock anger which used to hang in pride of place in his house in Ringmer until his executors passed it on to me after his death.

My contract for 1960 covered all the back-stage requirements for *Falstaff, I Puritani, Der Rosenkavalier, Don Giovanni, La Cenerentola, Die Zauberflöte* as well as being Assistant Chorus Master and to coach all the operas except *Falstaff*, with which, fortuitously, I was unfamiliar. Inevitably Jani scheduled me to 'coach' Sesto Bruscantini in Master Ford, a role he had performed many times so I could add little to his understanding of the character but somehow fumbled my way through the fiendishly difficult piano part. *Falstaff* was televised as an outside broadcast after the Festival and I conducted the camera rehearsals to spare Maestro Gui but he sat behind me and clapped the beats. Needless to say, Jani was doing the same with his feet, which didn't coincide with either Gui or me. For *I Puritani*, I conducted a whole

The close up full frontal of me during a rehearsal of Britten's *Let's make an opera*, 1979, for The State Opera of South Australia.

Curtain call for Michael Tippett's *Midsummer Marriage* at the Adelaide festival in 1978. The cast from left to right: Ruth Gurner, Thomas Edmunds, Carolyn Vaughan, Michael Tippett, Myer Fredman, Marilyn Richardson (hidden), Raimund Herincx, Gregory Dempsey, Susan Kessler and Keith Hempton.

array of instruments backstage: side drums, four horns, organ and I had to climb up a lighting pole to relay the beat to the chorus from where it was an ideal position to hear Joan Sutherland for the first time. My next encounter with *La Stupenda* was in a doctor's waiting room in Adelaide, South Australia. I was sitting alone waiting to be seen when in walked Dame Joan who sat down opposite and began to knit. I finally picked up enough courage to ask if she remembered me and she certainly did. Some years later we were co-adjudicators for the Sun Aria competition in Sydney and more recently, when Opera Australia celebrated its fiftieth anniversary, Dame Joan took centre stage once more. This time to sing *Happy Birthday to You* surrounded by the entire company but it was the only time I had the privilege of conducting for her.

Sir Thomas Beecham was due to conduct *Die Zauberflöte* but as his health was beginning to fail the young Colin Davis was engaged in his place. My involvement in the opera, being the 'commissar of backstage duties', was to conduct a stage manager's playing of the enormous thunder drum that had been especially constructed for *Macbeth* back in 1939. Jani never allowed his music staff to play it as our hands were sacrosanct so I had to follow his carefully annotated score that indicated distant, close and intermittent rolls, their duration and the precise number of thunder claps. We had to be in complete darkness so I held a torch in one hand and turned the pages of Jani's instructions as best I could. Being way at the back of the stage it was difficult to hear the spoken dialogue so it was very easy for a tremendous thunderclap to occur in the wrong place. Since that time, such stage effects are electronically controlled from the prompt corner, which is a pity in some ways as fledgling conductors benefit from working in difficult conditions and appreciating the perpetual turmoil back-stage.

When the BBC organised a conducting competition to be televised on the *Monitor* programme, I applied with a recommendation from Jani who wrote, '*I consider Mr. Fredman as steady very dutiful and resourceful in personality with great musical abilities and gifts as a conductor'*. Peter's recommendation was equally complimentary, *'I consider him to be a young conductor of more than ordinary talent, a conscientious and understanding musician, and also a person of real integrity'*. Their perspicacity has certainly borne fruit, especially *'dutiful and resourceful and a person of real integrity'*, but I now realise that *integrity* has sometimes been to my disadvantage. The orchestra was the New Philharmonia and the formidable panel of judges consisted of Carlo Maria Giulini, Otto Klemperer, Sir Adrian Boult and Walter Legge. Few of us had ever conducted a professional orchestra never mind on live television in front of such illustrious maestri. We each conducted a movement from Beethoven's *Second Symphony* and once again I failed to achieve a place in the first three. Meanwhile Glyndebourne had initiated a policy of engaging understudies due to the increasing strain imposed on opera singers who now spent much of their energy jetting round the world and, consequently were becoming prone to viruses and infections of one sort or another and compelled to cancel engagements. Glyndebourne's understudy casts were drawn from the young choristers. I was given overall responsibility and at first they only had music calls but a year or so later production rehearsals were added, and this in turn led to understudy 'showings' with minimal sets and costumes. The idea of a young company to exploit their talent was then formulated and in 1968, Glyndebourne Touring Opera came into being with me as its first Musical Director. Soon after that, Peter was appointed Chorus Director at the BBC and I took over the Glyndebourne Chorus for revivals of *L'elisir d'amore, Figaro* and *Così fan tutte* and the new productions of *Pelléas et Mélisande* and *L'incoronazione di Poppea*. When John Pritchard came to rehearse the men's chorus in *Poppea* he wanted them to sing a difficult unison ornament different to how I had trained them, so in the few remaining rehearsals they had to unlearn what they had memorised and implant the new version. Then when *Poppea* was revived the following year, I assiduously rehearsed what John had wanted only to find that he had changed his mind: a typical predicament for all Chorus Masters. After the season was over, *Il barbiere di Siviglia* was recorded and as a result of singing too much when I was rehearsing the Chorus I developed a sore throat and lost my voice – an embarrassing conclusion to my first season as Chorus Master!

My new position entailed holding regular auditions so I heard three hundred or more hopeful young singers every winter who tended to be either very good, very bad or indeterminate with the latter being in the majority. One baritone brought Leporello's Catalogue Aria from *Don Giovanni* and proceeded to sing it while holding an imaginary notebook in which he wrote the names of the Don's conquests: he remembered to turn every page but only managed to coincide with the music every eighth or ninth bar! There was always a sizeable Australian contingent (though not every one was a potential Joan Sutherland) so I asked Geoffrey Parsons, who came from Sydney, if there was a reason why? With a twinkle in his eye Geoffrey said that it was because Australians have to perpetually squint at the sun which opens the resonating chambers in the mask of the face!

A Memorial Service was held in Westminster Abbey for John Christie, Glyndebourne's founder, for which Gui conducted Mozart's Requiem and I prepared the chorus. A few weeks afterwards a letter arrived from George Christie with a photo of his father in an inscribed silver frame. *'The whole service was for me extremely beautiful – but the performance of the Requiem was particularly so and for this I am to a very large extent grateful to you. The chorus was really superb – even the Abbey's acoustics could not disguise this. It was indeed kind of you to have taken such great trouble to have trained and prepared them so excellently and to have given up so much time to do this. The Abbey deserved to be packed to have such a wonderful performance in it. You could not have paid a more generous nor finer tribute to my father and I am profoundly grateful.'* That same year saw my debut on the concert platform with the Bournemouth Symphony Orchestra and the concert was repeated in Weston-Super-Mare where a ship's funnel added its own colourful contribution to the orchestration of Sibelius' *Second Symphony*.

Fidelio was revived the following season (1963) and because Beethoven's writing is actually unvocal, especially for sopranos and tenors, and can easily damage young voices, I rehearsed down a fourth and only gradually worked my way up through every key to his original pitch. Spike Hughes, in his history of the Sussex opera house *Glyndebourne*, wrote *'The Glyndebourne Festival Chorus made a special hit of its own in the last scene of the work, when it sang with an attack and rhythmic bite instilled into it by its new Chorus Master Myer Fredman which was sadly lacking in the orchestra pit and elsewhere'*. That year also saw my Glyndebourne debut as a conductor with two performances of *Le nozze di Figaro* because Silvio Varviso asked to be released from his last performances due to an unexpected recording offer for him, so it was too late to engage another 'name' conductor. I was granted one orchestral rehearsal without the cast yet Jani still decided to give me notes on my performance during the Interval. He obviously couldn't wait for the opera to finish but when it did, I went out to take my curtain call and slid, feet first into the prompt box leaving only my head and shoulders visible: an auspicious debut!

During the winter I conducted my first *Don Giovanni* (but not at Glyndebourne). On the opening night, as the curtain rose on the cemetery scene, the audience were able to see the Commendatore's statue mounting his horse but that was only the beginning. Elvira failed to appear on stage in the Finale to Act II so the Don, Leporello and I improvised until she finally arrived in time to make her exit, bumped into the statue and let out a faint squawk instead of the customary scream. Another engagement was assisting John Pritchard with the Liverpool Philharmonic (now the Royal) in a programme devoted to contemporary music as part of his *Musica Viva* series. I rehearsed Alban Berg's *Chamber Concerto for Violin, Piano and Wind* for John while he was away conducting on the Continent and when he arrived for the rehearsal on the morning of the concert and conducted the performance, it was as if he had rehearsed it solidly for a week. John had the amazing ability of conducting as if he was extemporising yet I have no doubt he must have thoroughly studied the score beforehand. Whereas some conductors arrive promptly for a ten o'clock rehearsal then slave away for three hours but achieve little, John would often arrive late, finish early yet create a performance of great beauty. After one of the *Musica Viva* concerts I returned to London on the over-night sleeper and, after settling down for the night a Colonel Blimp character came into the double compartment. Silence reigned for a while and then he said, *'Are you in commerce?'* To which I replied, *'No, I am a musician.'* More silence until, *'Do you know David Wilcox?' 'No, I know his name of course though I've never worked with him.'* More silence then he gave me his stamp of approval, *'He was my adjutant during the war, damned good map reader!'* On that note our conversation ended but I suppose that for some of the Establishment then if not now, musicians who could read a map must be alright as, after all, reading a full score is not that unlike reading a map! I was told later about a conducting competition in Liverpool (which I hadn't entered) that the winner was a young Indian called Zubin Mehta who, apparently, was the best of a rather mediocre bunch.

The 1965 Glyndebourne season proved to be a particularly busy one for me. I was the sostituo conductor (substitute conductor) for Donizetti's *Anna Bolena* and Gui's cover for Cimarosa's *Il matrimonio segreto* which was to open the season. The opening night would be on May 16 and on the previous night I was scheduled to make my Royal Festival Hall debut with Robert Still's new *Sinfonia*, Beethoven's *Fourth Piano Concerto* and Sibelius' *Fifth Symphony*. I knew all the scores very well but had never conducted them and, knowing that the concerto is difficult to co-ordinate with the soloist in places, I phoned Clifford Curzon who, I had been told, was a rather prickly character. He virtually shouted down the phone, *'What! You want to go through the concerto with me?'* then he softened *'It's been a long time since a conductor bothered to do so, I would be delighted'*. We spent a whole afternoon comparing various editions and pointing out the places where he would give me the nod to bring in the orchestra.

Back at Glyndebourne I conducted the early rehearsals of *Il matrimonio segreto* because Gui cabled Glyndebourne that he would be arriving late as his wife had fallen ill. I didn't know a note of this rarely performed opera and sight-read it, but after a week went by Gui telegraphed a further delay so I took the orchestra rehearsals and then he cabled again to say that he would only arrive after the opening night. This meant that I would be conducting the first three or four performances yet I hadn't properly digested the score, an unforgivable error on my part. My Festival Hall debut would fall between the Public Dress Rehearsal and the opening night but I was already exhausted and, to make matters worse, I hadn't booked into a hotel to rest before the concert but tried to sleep (and failed) on a friend's settee. It must have been an uninspired concert and certainly not the success my London debut ought to have been but Robert asked me to record his *Sinfonia* not long after. The recording only took the first of the two scheduled sessions so Mr. Itter — Lyrita's manager — suggested I use the second one for whatever I liked from works he had ready for such an eventuality. I chose Arthur Benjamin's *Overture to an Italian Comedy*, which I didn't know and Delius' *The Walk to the Paradise Garden* and found myself recording Delius, who had been the prerogative of none other than Sir Thomas Beecham, with the Royal Philharmonic, his orchestra.

When Gui finally arrived at Glyndebourne he took over *Il matrimonio segreto* and then conducted *Le nozze di Figaro*, lingering over every phrase with so much love and affection that the opera lasted far longer than usual. Gérard Souzay and Montserrat Caballé were the Count and Countess but at the start of the second performance it was discovered that Souzay had vanished from his dressing room and returned to France so the understudy had to be hastily fitted into Souzay's costume albeit that the Overture had already started. Before the next performance, Caballé had fallen ill so her understudy went on and Michel Roux took over the Count, and it was all becoming too much for the ageing Maestro. He decided to withdraw until everything settled down and I took over without rehearsal, but this was to create yet further chaos. This was because the restaurant caterers – who timed the dinner to coincide with the conclusion of the second act – were caught completely unawares by my quicker tempi, which had lopped twenty minutes off the playing time. In his book, Spike Hughes wrote, *'Once more, Myer Fredman (still in his spare time, Chorus Master) took over, and in the course of seven days conducted three performances of* Figaro *and three of* Anna Bolena *(Gavazzeni had fulfilled his contract and returned to Italy). The reason Mr. Fredman rested on the seventh day had nothing to do with working to Mosaic rule. There was no performance that night.'*

In the autumn I conducted in a season of quite a different calibre to that which I was now accustomed: *La Bohème* in Torquay where I had grown up and only a stone's throw from where I had first seen the same opera in that bitterly cold winter of 1948. The company could only afford minimal rehearsals so my one and only orchestral rehearsal was in Eastbourne, the single rehearsal with the stage was in Torquay, five hundred or so miles away. The Glyndebourne season included *Die Zauberflöte* in which George Shirley – the Afro-American tenor – sang Tamino who, on hearing the men's chorus in Act II said *'Gee, what a sound, it's enough to make your hair stand up straight and with me, that takes some doing.'* George also created something of a problem in that Mozart and Schikaneder had conceived Monostatos as the embodiment of evil and therefore black: the solution was to give Tamino green hair! As *Die Zauberflöte* has a strong association with Freemasonry, the producer assumed that Sarastro's household would have been male only and therefore he requested the ladies in the chorus to wear beards, but they felt sexually rather degraded as a result. In fact, as both Mozart and Schikaneder were Freemasons, they would have been well aware of female Lodges and that after undergoing certain trials, the sexes were allowed to mingle as mirrored in the trials of Fire and Water in the opera! Whenever Glyndebourne programmed *Die Zauberflöte*, Jani would hold what we dubbed 'permutation auditions' for the Damen and Knaben (Ladies and Boys). About twenty sopranos and altos would be brought together for Jani, Martin Isepp and myself to hear them three at a time and in different permutations until Jani was satisfied that he had found the perfect combination. By the time the season came around four months later, the results for some explicable reason, were not always as perfect as they had seemed at the time. Only recently has Glyndebourne considered using real boys for the Knaben. It was also the year that Jani invited a female to join the music staff for the first time, so women's lib. had finally arrived in Sussex.

Being a Festival Opera rather than a permanent company, the chorus was disbanded between seasons but I managed to obtain work for them in two BBC television operas, *Carmen* and *La traviata*. At that time, the BBC recorded opera visually in a studio at the Television Centre while the orchestra and conductor played the score at the other end of London. I relayed Charles Mackerras' beat for the singers while moving around the studio with the cameras, avoiding the cables or being caught on camera (hopefully), while the orchestral sound was fed into us at the lowest possible volume to avoid spilling into the studio's microphones. The technique was abandoned a few years later thanks to Benjamin Britten who refused to compose an opera for television unless the conductor, orchestra and singers were in the same studio: the result was *Owen Wingrave*. It was about that time that I began to teach conducting as I was asked to help a young composer, John Tavener, who was to conduct his choral and orchestral work, *The Whale*. The complex score was far too difficult to play on the piano so we worked in complete silence and I quickly discovered that it was an excellent way to develop a talent as I had to see the conductor's inner intentions emanating from the tip of the baton.

That same year I was invited to conduct at the Wexford Festival for the first time. Despite having little financial backing, the Festival had attracted international singers and had been producing some remarkable performances on the smallest of shoestrings. One such production had nevertheless played havoc with Bellini's *I Puritani* as the opera's final scene was completely cut because it depicted Oliver Cromwell and his army relieving the Protestant garrison from the marauding Catholics! The opera I conducted was Auber's amusing *Fra Diavolo*, on which Hollywood had based a film starring Abbott and Costello, but all I can remember was that the comprimario tenor persistently propositioned me for engagements elsewhere.

When Glyndebourne toured Scandinavia in the autumn of 1967 the Norwegian Opera invited me to join their conducting staff, but I turned down the offer because the launch of Glyndebourne Touring Opera was in the offing. Then after Copenhagen, I flew to Toronto to work in the Opera School of the Royal Conservatory where the Director was none other than Boyd Neel, who had conducted John Christie's first attempt at full-scale opera in Tunbridge Wells where I now lived. Boyd invited me to join his staff which I had to turn down for the same reasons as in Oslo, but resulting from the Scandinavian tour I was invited to conduct the Malmö Symphony Orchestra in a programme which would include the Violin Concerto by Sibelius. I decided that the rest of the programme should promote English music so to open I chose the *Divertimento* by Lennox Berkeley and to close, Vaughan-Williams' very dissonant *Fourth Symphony*. The rehearsals went very well and I got the impression from the General Manager that I would be invited to fill the vacant position of Music Director, but that was not to be. When the violinist arrived to rehearse on the morning of the concert, she informed me in no uncertain terms that she had waited for me at her hotel the previous evening to talk through the concerto but I had failed to appear. It was a serious mistake on my part for I was having dinner at the home of the Concert Master, and, being confident of the imminent appointment, had forgotten to phone her. At the rehearsal she stopped all the time to correct the orchestra for their slightest imperfection and during the performance, our collaboration – or lack of it – was, to say the least, very tense. She must have made it her business to denigrate me with the orchestra's management and the Stockholm agent so I never received an invitation for a return engagement. To add insult to injury, the Malmö music critic had damned the concert with *'we all know that England is the home of Divertimenti and Serenades!'* I certainly didn't.

It was about that same time that I met Havergal Brian after reading his biography and who, like my wife, hailed from Stoke on Trent, affectionately known as the Potteries. He was already in his nineties yet remarkably alert, having composed an incredible number of symphonies and other works during the previous ten years and there were still more to come. The following week, the BBC was to record his Violin Concerto for a future broadcast and he invited me to come to the studio where I met Robert Simpson the programme's producer and very much a composer in his own right. As a result of that meeting, Bob and I developed a strong friendship over the years and I conducted a number of Brian premières as well as music by other composers that had been overlooked. The *Second Symphony* of Max Bruch, Dvorák's *First Symphony* and the *Serenades* and *Humouresques* by Sibelius for Solo Violin and orchestra were among the forgotten works, but a particular curiosity was Wagner's <u>three</u> versions of his Venesburg music for *Tannhäuser*. The third version is usually performed today but his first attempt sounds like Donizetti and the second, a little more Wagnerian but still very foursquare. Bob intimated to me after a number of years of our friendship that I took as a great compliment *'Myer, you're different from other conductors, you're not an ego-centric megalomaniac!'*

The year 1968 was particularly exciting for two reasons. During the season I conducted performances of Tchaikovsky's *Eugene Onegin*, which was a completely new to me and was to become a special favourite. It did present a problem, however, because of Glyndebourne's policy of opera always being sung in the original language and I was unable to sense the singer's phrasing and breathing from the Cyrillic text. The other reason was that Glyndebourne Touring Opera was launched to take some of the Festival productions to the major cities so that the general population had the opportunity to enjoy them and, equally important, to provide an outlet for up and coming young performers. Our tour opened in Newcastle-upon-Tyne then on to Liverpool, Manchester, Sheffield and Oxford with the Northern Sinfonia in the pit (when there was one), and the company was a great success. I conducted two performances of *Don Giovanni* and two of *Die Zauberflöte* each and every week so they were a good test of my stamina. Raymond Leppard conducted his own realisation of Cavalli's *L'Ormindo* and *L'elisir d'amore* was conducted by Kenneth Montgomery. The operas were performed in the same order in each city except in Manchester where the two Mozart operas were reversed. But the three trombonists, having forgotten the switch, assumed that *Don Giovanni* would be first. As brass players always know the precise moment when to enter the pit they had gone to a cinema knowing they would be out in time to play in Act II but unfortunately for them it was *Die Zauberflöte* in which the trombones play at the opening of the Overture. When I entered the pit, their seats were unoccupied and we had to delay the start for quite some time till they arrived. Afterwards they were suitably admonished, but not sacked.

Sir Michael Redgrave's beautiful and evocative production of *Werther* was revived in the 1969 Festival with me as the conductor but the tenor in the principal role sweated profusely, stood centre-stage most of the time and never took his eyes off me. GTO included Massenet's opera that year and during the concluding pages to Act I, the cinema's usherette complete with her tray of cigarettes, confectionery and ice-cream, appeared from under the stage, made her way through the orchestra, and stood at the front of the auditorium ready for the Interval. She was totally unconcerned about there being an orchestra behind her or even that an opera was being performed rather than a film: she was doing what she was paid to do. Other GTO tours also had their fair share of off-stage dramas as when the curtain came down on *Macbeth* in Manchester. I complimented the Stage Manager on the vivid realism of the battle scene only to be told *'That's because the arc lights caught fire'*. By the time we had arrived in Bristol, the copies of the English translation of *Eugene Onegin* had all been sold out so our Stage Director narrated the plot over the theatre's speaker system while the sets were being changed. Having previously been an actor, he revelled in his performance but one night as we waited on stage the theatre manager told us that there had been a bomb scare. The Stage Director was far too busy at the microphone to register the fact until finally the manager grabbed it and reassured the audience. I then went into the pit, raised my arms to conduct, and cheekily looked for the bomb under the music stand. Then there was the instance of arriving in Newcastle only to discover that the orchestral parts of *Così fan tutte* were still in Oxford.

At the next Wexford Festival I conducted Verdi's early opera, *Luisa Miller*, but the soprano had to withdraw at the last minute due to illness and fortunately another was found who actually knew this rarely performed opera. The set had been designed as a series of kaleidoscopic mirrors, which was a novel idea but as it reflected the stage lighting into the pit I was perpetually blinded when I looked up. If that wasn't enough, the producer decided that a pair of Irish wolfhounds would be in keeping with the character of the Duchess and I received the full flavour of their unique aroma. Fate had something worse in store for me when I hired a car to drive up to Dublin Airport to collect my wife on the morning of the opening night. I set off with not a care in the world, then, without warning, the car went out of control and turned upside down; it took me quite a while to extricate myself. I staggered around looking for my glasses (found them) when a member of the Festival Committee found me and took me back to Wexford to the Sisters of Charity Hospital. I was x-rayed and heavily sedated; there were no bones broken though my neck and shoulders were badly bruised. The Festival's Artistic Director came to see me and was naturally concerned about the performance taking place so he delicately enquired *'Can you conduct tonight?'* to which I could only mumble *'I'll try'*. A doctor froze my arms at each Interval but when I made any strong gesture, the pain was excruciating. After the performance I was taken back to the hospital with a present of a bottle of whisky (Irish of course) which the nun on night duty and I swigged all night. After ten days of physiotherapy and managing somehow to conduct the remaining performances I was discharged. Jani phoned from England, of course, to remind me that we had music staff auditions as soon as I returned.

Thanks to the Lyrita recordings of Still, Delius and Benjamin, Mr. Itter phoned to ask if I knew the *First Symphony* of Arnold Bax and would I consider recording it in ten days' time. Ten days was very short notice but he sent the score round to me by express post and after reading it, I accepted. He instantly proposed Bax's *Second Symphony* as well so, in for a penny in for a pound even though I could only have five sessions to record both. Only one musician in the entire London Philharmonic Orchestra had ever played either of them so we needed time to become familiar with the style. Rehearsing and recording the first movement of the *First Symphony* with re-takes took so long that by the time we reached the last movement of the *Second Symphony* only a half session remained to read it through once before the red light went on to record it in one take. Ken Russell, the producer of the famous television programmes about Elgar and Delius, had sponsored the recordings and later wrote to me, *'I have had one run through of the Bax symphonies which contain many exciting moments. Considering the circumstances, I think you did a remarkably fine job on them – congratulations. Doubtless, we will be in touch at some future date, until then – all the best.'*

Sir John Barbirolli died while conducting in Japan during the 1970 Glyndebourne season, so John Pritchard flew out to replace him and I conducted the remaining performances of *Eugene Onegin* and Rossini's *Il turco in Italia* as well as my own series of *Die Zauberflöte*. That summer I sight read a stage with orchestra rehearsal of Cavalli's *La Calisto* because Raymond Leppard was delayed in South America and after the season I became Otto Klemperer's assistant for his recording of *Così fan tutte*. I was engaged to warm up the Philharmonia Orchestra at the beginning of each session so I went to his hotel to go through the score with him, but he never mentioned anything about the score. Instead he remarked that I looked like Mahler as a young man which was rather flattering, though I have never noticed the likeness. My first assignment turned out to be the Overture and knowing of his reputation for slow tempi, I conducted it at a funereal pace but when he arrived, he took if far faster than I ever thought possible. He slowed down the tempo quite considerably, however, after he listened to a take in the recording booth. The cast was Lucia Popp, Yvonne Minton, Luigi Alva and Geraint Evans, who of course knew the opera inside out, but Klemperer decided to record Act II without any of the usual cuts so I had to rehearse them that morning in music they had never previously performed. The sessions provided a fantastic opportunity to watch him in action and to try to fathom out how the orchestra followed his gestures which appeared to be uncoordinated and bore little relation to the music. Some of the musicians told me that they couldn't follow him either but there was no doubt that the orchestra sensed what *emanated* from him: a salutary lesson as to what the art of conducting is all about.

At the next Camden Festival I conducted *Fennimore & Gerda*, a one-act opera by Delius. It was its first ever production in England because apart from the well known Intermezzi which Beecham had often performed, he never conducted the opera: apparently Delius and Peter Warlock are said to have adversely criticised his British National Opera Company. When I studied the score I discovered some perplexing anomalies so I went to see Eric Fenby, Delius' amanuensis, who told me that 'Fred' would finish off working for the day and would begin writing the next morning quite oblivious of his notation of the previous day so that the time signature 4/2 might become 4/4 or vice versa. I cautiously suggested that perhaps Delius had been a highly gifted amateur but Fenby put it slightly differently: *'Fred was the least professional of composers'* and though an ardent champion of the composer he added, *'Fred couldn't write for the harp'*. He also told me something else that Delius had said of great importance, *'that if you feel the music with passion and intensity, it's bound to be right'*. The producer for *Fennimore* had been connected with some of Delius' inner circle, among them Bernard van Dieren, a composer who had intrigued me ever since I first read Constant Lambert's fascinating book *Music Ho!* It turned out that Bernard van Dieren's son was living in Tunbridge Wells just a few streets away from where I lived, so naturally I went to see him. His garage was full of tea chests containing his father's scores, including *The Chinese Symphony* for which Peter Warlock had copied the score and parts for a performance that Constant Lambert conducted in the 1930s. During our rehearsals the singers were finding the style of Delius unlike any other they had previously experienced so I told them what Fenby had said, that his music continuously ebbs and flows and may even do so drastically from one performance to the next. The producer took that to mean that I would radically distort the music at each performance so unknown to us all, he collected up the orchestral parts and disappeared with them just before the Dress Rehearsal. I received an express letter from his solicitor demanding me to sign a lawyer's affidavit to the effect that I wouldn't change one single tempo. I naturally refused to sign it and in the end, the parts were returned and the Dress Rehearsal began.

Jani retired from Glyndebourne after the 1970 season was over and recommended me to be his successor, so the question arose as to my title. He had been *Head of Music Staff and Preparation*, so it would have been unethical for me to prepare an opera for another conductor. I proposed *First Conductor and Head of Music Staff* as being comparable to *Erste Kapellmeister* in German, meaning the conductor immediately under the Musical Director. My suggestion was accepted but the title in English could be easily misinterpreted and John Pritchard, who had been appointed *Music Director* only the previous year, was understandably perturbed. Various alternatives were discussed but as none fully described my new position it remained as it was, or so I assumed. After appearing in the programme for the first two years as *First Conductor &*

Head of Music Staff, it was dropped but I only became aware of that after leaving Sussex.

I spent a month in Brussels working on Cavalli's *L'Ormindo* at the Theatre Monnaie in 1972 and between two of the performances I flew back to England for an out of town concert with the Royal Philharmonic Orchestra. The main work was the *Symphony No. 2* by Brahms which I had never conducted before. I had just begun to rehearse the symphony when I realised that the three-hour rehearsal was virtually over. I thanked the orchestra who seemed unduly grateful for some reason; I had forgotten to adjust my watch from Belgian to Greenwich Mean Time. I therefore conducted my first ever Brahms Symphony with only five minute's rehearsal! After *L'Ormindo* finished my wife and I flew to Warsaw and on to Poznan by train where I was to conduct *Rigoletto* and *Carmen*. As soon as I began to rehearse with the cast it was evident that, thanks to the communist regime, singers, like the rest of the population, had to work until the official retirement age regardless as to whether they had voices or not. The Concert Master invited us home one evening but warned us not to talk in the taxi in case the driver was an informer. When we arrived, he and his wife plied us with quantities of Polish vodka, which is far stronger than the Russian variety. When we were sufficiently inebriated, he took Jeanne into another room leaving his wife with me and then, when we swapped partners I realised why. He needed to talk to me, *'I love my wife but I can't stand the regime so can you get me out of the country?'* I said I would try when we returned to England but I didn't pursue the matter as I had been warned that such attempts might land me in serious trouble; I later heard that he was leading an orchestra in Iran. In Lodz (pronounced Wootch) I conducted my first ever *Madama Butterfly* after having had only one rehearsal with the singers and none with the orchestra. The theatre had only recently been built and the conductor's rostrum was as complex as a control desk in a recording studio with a vast array of buttons and switches. Just before the off-stage humming chorus was due to begin, a whole bank of arc lights came on and focused on me. I instantaneously assumed that I was going to be interrogated but it was only for the offstage conductor to see me clearly. While in Lodz, I asked to hear whoever wanted to sing for me in case there were any singers suitable for Glyndebourne and got into trouble as a result. I had failed to praise a particular soprano who, it turned out, was the wife of the local communist bigwig! After Poland, Wexford was a great relief with its adequate rehearsals, no politics and no repeat performance of a car crash. Instead I conducted Puccini's *La Rondine* which Spike Hughes once wittily described as *'much better than people lead me to believe, but unfortunately not quite as good as one hopes'*.

Having suggested Bernard van Dieren's *Chinese Symphony* and Elgar's forgotten early oratorio *Lux Christi* to the BBC, I conducted both works for a studio broadcast from Manchester and wrote to Sir Adrian Boult that he might care to listen to the broadcast. Sir Adrian was a great Elgarian and had known the composer but most probably had never conducted *Lux Christi*. A courteous letter arrived from him by return post to say that unfortunately he was unable to hear the broadcast but would I like to have lunch with him some time. I fixed a date with his secretary for the day after my return from engagements in Romania and when I arrived home, she phoned to say that the elevator in the Wigmore Studios had broken down. I shouldn't attempt to climb the stairs to his studio on the top floor, Sir Adrian would come down to meet me. This was a great conductor in his eighties yet still prepared to descend to my level (in both senses) and off we went to his favourite restaurant on the top floor of the John Lewis department store in Oxford Street. He suggested a glass of sherry before lunch and while we ate, we chatted. But he wouldn't be drawn about his association with either Elgar or Vaughan-Williams, and instead enthused about his forthcoming recordings of Wagner excerpts and his student days in Leipzig. After lunch he politely asked whether I might be interested in having some lessons from him even though I was already an established conductor, as he was most concerned about the current generation of conductors who appeared to know little of the basic craft. I received his book through the post shortly afterwards and practised some of the exercises before returning to the Wigmore Studios where he gave me a lesson for an hour or so. I know of no conductor who holds the baton between forefinger and thumb as did Sir Adrian but nevertheless I learnt a great deal about clarity and keeping everything simple.

My Romanian visit had been in April by which time the snow-ploughs had been put away for the summer, but on the very day I arrived, Bucharest ground to a halt in a totally unexpected blizzard. As there was no transport of any kind I had to walk to the theatre for the rehearsals and the performance and after wading through the slush in my tails and patent shoes I conducted *Don Giovanni* with very cold wet feet. I then went by train to Cluz, in the region where Bartók had collected many folk songs. Though relatively small, the city had two splendid opera houses, one for the Romanian-speaking population and the other for the Hungarian. One Sunday when free of a rehearsal I went to a matinée of Mozart's *Die Entführung aus dem Serail* in the Romanian house where the audience seemed to be comprised of parents and children who revelled in booing Osmin because he epitomised the long since departed Ottoman invader. In the Hungarian opera house I conducted *La Bohème* after the usual one rehearsal with the singers and none with the orchestra, but just before the performance the Rodolfo fell sick and a Romanian tenor sang the role. The opera was therefore sung in two languages but that didn't worry me as I 'heard' it in Italian anyway, but during the performance I found myself in an awkward predicament. Having reached the nineteenth bar in Act 2 (the Café Momus) where the chorus should start to sing, the curtain was still down. Should I stop or go on? In a split second decision I decided to continue and ten bars later the curtain rose to save us all from acute embarrassment or so I thought. After the performance I tactfully raised the subject with the producer who replied *'Don't you know this opera?'* I was flabbergasted, *'Of course I do'*. *'Well, where does Puccini indicate the curtain to rise?'* I opened my score and there, sure enough, 'Si alza il Sipario' is printed over bar twenty-eight, ten bars <u>after</u> the chorus begins to sing. In Puccini's time it would have been a brilliant theatrical effect but it's now considered rather passé, at least in the West.

The position of Erste Kapellmeister at the Hamburg State Opera had become vacant so I went over to conduct a performance of *Carmen* as my audition. I had been informed that it would be performed in the original edition which I took to mean Bizet's original score and as I fortunately had a copy I studied far more of the music than is normally performed today. When I arrived in Hamburg I discovered that 'original' meant that it would be sung in French and not German so my extra study had been in vain. I entered the pit, shook hands and said *Guten Abend* to the Leader and away we went. Afterwards, an assistant administrator in the wings said 'thank you' and that was that: I returned to my lonely hotel room and flew back to London the following morning. A month or so later I received the news that they had liked my work but the current incumbent had changed his mind and would not be vacating the position. As it happened not being offered the position was all for the good for during our second Glyndebourne visit to Copenhagen I received two invitations on the same day. The first was from Brussels for *Die Zauberflöte* at the Monnaie and the second from the Australian Opera for *Il barbiere di Siviglia* as part of the opening season at the Sydney Opera House. Moran Caplat's advice was to accept Brussels, it being only an hour or so away, whereas Australia was at the other end of the world. I finally decided on Sydney, however, out of curiosity and, as a result, my metaphorical toss of a coin led to a complete change of life for my family and myself. Ironically, my Australian cousins had been in England only a few months before and had said *'Ever thought of coming to Australia?'* to which my very definite answer was *'No, that will never happen'*. After Copenhagen and GTO, I went to Paris at very short notice to conduct a broadcast of *Hansel und Gretel* for ORTF as the contracted German conductor had fallen ill and there was no French chef d'orchestre available who knew the opera. Though I had never conducted the complete opera I knew many of the scenes from my student days and quickly learnt the remainder, flew to Paris and filled in the usual entry documents. The recording took place on the stage of the Opera Comique (then used as a night-club) and during one of the coffee breaks I explored the foyers and realised that this was the theatre in which operas by Massenet, Gounod, Bizet and Debussy had all received their premières. When I told the orchestra what an honour it was for me to work in that theatre some of the players merely shrugged their shoulders but whether through the famous Parisian indifference or my abuse of the French language I have no idea!

For our *Barber of Seville*, which in Sydney would be sung in English, John Cox and I agreed about modelling the set on the Prince Regent Pavilion in Brighton as it was in keeping with Rossini's sense of humour as well as the period in which he lived. One of the reviews mentioned *'Myer Fredman, who has a fine reputation from Glyndebourne, performed miracles with the Elizabethan Trust Sydney Orchestra. Light, mercurial, and stylish playing gave the opera the bubbling impetus it deserves.'* Jani in retirement was regularly coaching for the Australian Opera so he came to the opening night but stormed past me after the performance without saying one word: it was obvious that something had displeased him. When I confronted the oracle his retort was simple, *'You conducted Rossini as if he was Mozart'*: needless to say he was right as usual, despite the rave review. During the rehearsals I had seen a newspaper advertisement describing a position that looked decidedly interesting so I explored it further. The Manager of the New Opera Company in Adelaide, Justin Macdonnell, came over to discuss the matter with me, and as Jeanne had arrived for a short holiday, we were both invited to Adelaide which was in the middle of its regular Arts Festival. Janácek's *The Adventures of Mr. Broucek* was being performed in the Festival Theatre with the Adelaide Symphony Orchestra in the pit and I also met a number of people including Anthony Steele, Director of both the Adelaide Festival and the Theatre. To work in Adelaide would obviously be exciting and we returned to Sydney with the impression that the position would be offered in due course. Jeanne flew back to England and I flew on to Phoenix to conduct *The Tales of Hoffmann* for the University of Arizona's Opera Department. Some time elapsed before the New Opera Company's Board of Directors confirmed my appointment because the position had actually been advertised with a young Australian in mind and, being a newly created company from a semi-amateur background, they hadn't considered the likelihood that someone of my calibre might be interested. When their offer finally reached me in Phoenix, I wrote to Jani and received a telegram from Moran asking for confirmation that I would be leaving Glyndebourne to which my cryptic reply was *'Boomerangs make excellent batons'*. As if in a French farce, a letter also arrived from Paris, not with an offer but stating that on my entry documents the previous year, I had failed to disclose the maiden name of my wife's mother!

Apart from conducting *The Visit of the Old Lady* at Glyndebourne and GTO it took most of 1974 to organise our permanent move to Australia because I believed that to properly establish the new company in Adelaide, I had to live as well as work there. Justin Macdonnell came over to Tunbridge Wells and we mapped out a five-year plan to include Baroque, Mozart, Romantic, Contemporary opera and Music Theatre, and to create a contemporary music ensemble which would also be the core of our opera orchestra. Anthony Steele, on a visit to London, asked me to form an equivalent of the Edinburgh Festival Choir so what with laying the foundations of an opera company, a contemporary music ensemble and the training of a virtuoso choir, I felt that my cup had runneth over. After the curtain came down on my last performance at Glyndebourne, and knowing of my passion for the music of Elgar, I was presented with a bound copy of his *Pomp & Circumstance March No. 2* suitably bound; inside the cover was Elgar's autograph to his friend and mentor, A. J. Jaeger, 1907. Glyndebourne's Dance Director, Pauline Grant, gave me a vocal score of Rossini's *Otello* that had been owned by Mahler and inside was her farewell, *'I want you to have something special. It has been marvellous working with you and you have taught me so much while carefully appearing not to be doing so.'* Spike Hughes autographed his recently published book *Glyndebourne* with an accompanying letter that began *'Carissimo Maestro ed amico'* and ended with *'For purely selfish reasons I find so few people around these days who talk about music the way I understand, and that's something I shall miss when you go to Australia.'* GTO presented me with a pair of wine decanter holders that grace our sideboard thirty-one years later and so ended fifteen years of association with Glyndebourne. Perhaps it was too long but considering my initial lack of self-confidence and my progression from Repetiteur to Chorus Master – Assistant Conductor – Conductor in my own right – First Conductor & Head of Music Staff and Musical Director of the Touring Company I had certainly come a long way. Each step may have been expediency on Glyndebourne's part, but as Moran Caplat once observed, *'it's not a matter of engaging the best people, but engaging the least bad'*!

The Athens of the South

When we arrived in the 'Athens of the South' on the river Torrens, I discovered that neither the Festival Theatre nor the Adelaide Symphony Orchestra were connected with The New Opera Company apart from possible engagements for future Festivals. I also discovered that the New Opera Company's office was infested with cockroaches, red-back spiders and other lovers of opera; gone was the Sussex manor, its croquet lawns and Ha-Ha: in their place were rush matting on the floors and a non-existent music library. However, resilient as ever, I prophesied in a newspaper interview that *'Style is like electricity, in that we know how it works but not what it is, which means that we will virtually have to eat, sleep and breathe as an entity and then the ensemble feeling will evolve'*. A curious statement but what I meant was that style cannot be taught but is somehow rubbed off from close association with experienced artists. My intention was to model the company on what I had gleaned from Glyndebourne: ample preparation to allow young singers to grow and become the source from which the national company – the Australian Opera – would draw its future artists. *Eugene Onegin* had been planned to launch the new company but Justin had been sending telegrams to me in England during the last months expressing concern about diminishing finances, the result of Australian Federal and State Governments economic difficulties. *Onegin* was abandoned along with our vision of a contemporary music ensemble and so my Adelaide debut turned out to be a double-bill of Stravinsky's *The Soldier's Tale* produced by Justin and Bizet's *Dr Miracle* with piano accompaniment. When he was with us in Tunbridge Wells, Justin had mentioned that there was a desperate shortage of tenors, so I invited a Glyndebourne chorister, Dennis O'Neill, to join us and he jumped at the opportunity to further his career as a soloist. He was now our principal tenor for *Dr. Miracle* followed by *Così fan tutte*, *The Threepenny Opera* and Cimarosa's *The Secret Marriage*. Dennis then returned to what was to be a spectacular career in the Northern Hemisphere with the Welsh National Opera, Covent Garden and other national and international companies.

Despite our financial problems we were determined to keep Anthony Besch's production of *Così fan tutte* and Britten's *The Turn of the Screw* as planned and we performed them back to back. The orchestra for the Mozart came from the Elder Conservatorium students so I had to have an inordinate number of rehearsals as they had no experience at holding an exact tempo for more than a few bars at a time, nor did they realise that singers had to breathe. The harpsichord continuo was played by a sixteen-year old pianist from Sydney who Charles Mackerras had asked me to take under my wing. Peter Gruenberg's extemporised commentary on the stage drama was phenomenal and, after singing and acting in our next production a madrigal opera, he went to London for further study on the piano and advanced computer technology. He was unsure which career to follow but the last I heard was that he had become Head of the Music Staff with the San Francisco Opera. A review of our Mozart was distinctly encouraging for the new company. *'This Così moved with wit and charm, was visually quite ravishing and was shaped with infinite musical elegance. With this appointment New Opera have assured themselves of a fascinating musical future. Each of the four times I have heard Fredman conduct in Australia has been an illuminating experience. New Opera's* Così fan tutte *was an amazing first Mozart venture from a young company. One can even detect the rare beginnings of that ultimate Mozart joy, perfectly balance and blended ensemble singing.'* Another reviewer wrote, *'The special person behind the lovely stylish Mozart sound, delicately balanced in detail as fine as in the stage work is Myer Fredman. His control and refinement of the youthful Conservatorium chamber orchestra was most masterly, and he held the stage and pit together on a long graceful elastic beat.'* We received the National Critics Award for *Così fan tutte* as the best opera production in South Australia in 1975.

For the Britten, we enlisted the cream of Adelaide's musicians, including Jiri Tancibudek, one time Principal Oboist in the Czech Philharmonic Orchestra, Robert Cooper the leader of the Adelaide Symphony who had led the Covent Garden Orchestra for a while, and Dick Smith a superb percussionist of the calibre of Jimmy Blades. For Quint we had no less an artist than Ron Dowd who I vividly remembered from *Fidelio* and *Oedipus Rex* at Sadlers Wells during my student days. The theatre was Her Majesty's Theatre, potentially the right size for us, but it had seen better days, especially with respect to its lighting equipment. At one performance all the lights on stage and in the pit suddenly failed and I was just about to stop conducting when they came on again; a few minutes later the same thing happened, just as the soprano was about to launch into the Governess' aria in Act I. The soprano, who had an indefinite sense of rhythm, continued in the blackout without faltering for a moment, but as soon as the lights came on again she floundered badly.

By this time the company's finances were now decidedly low so our next production was a baroque madrigal opera by Banchieri, which didn't require an orchestra, coupled with a staging of Janáček's *The Diary of a Man who Disappeared* with piano and superbly performed by Ron Dowd. Out of the blue I received an invitation from GTO to return as a guest conductor but feeling that I could not be away from the company for any length of time, I declined and with that my link with Glyndebourne was finally severed. Adelaide had produced many singers over the years of whom the doyen was Arnold Matters who, after an illustrious career at Covent Garden, retired to Adelaide and was now teaching. Another was an ex-Glyndebourne and Sadlers Wells tenor, Kevin Miller, and a third was the contralto Mary Jarred who had created Mother Gooses in the first *The Rake's Progress* at Glyndebourne. Others with artistic connections were Sibelius' grandson who practised medicine and played in an amateur string quartet, and Stravinsky's niece who was involved in Adelaide's modern dance company. Robert Helpmann was born and bred not far away and a nineteenth-century tram driver who had been a great favourite with the local ladies returned to England and started collecting folk songs – none other than Cecil Sharp! Another eminent resident who at the outbreak of the Second World War was marooned in Australia was Henry Krips, the brother of Josef Krips whose London concerts I had attended during my Army years. Henry was a great exponent of Viennese Operetta but surprisingly, he adored English music; on one occasion we swapped concerts with Henry conducting my English programme, and I his Viennese repertoire. Not long afterwards he conducted Lehar's *The Land of Smiles* for The State Opera.

I quickly became aware of the 'tall poppy' syndrome which, being derived from the Australian myth of egalitarianism, I didn't fully understand at first. A tall poppy is a celebrity who has to be cut down to size and it's an attitude that seems to rear its head in all walks of life in Oz except of course sport. The syndrome started up almost immediately for me; why did he come to Australia? Why did he have to leave Glyndebourne (the haunt of 'silver tails' meaning the rich)? Is he here because he's not successful elsewhere and, worst of all, why hasn't an Australian being appointed? Such questions were probably the result of an artistic inferiority complex known as the 'cultural cringe' but hopefully when (rather than if) Australia becomes a Republic, they will completely evaporate. Another obstacle for me was that the ABC (Australian Broadcasting Corporation) had a virtual monopoly on music in Australia so it took quite a while before I was invited to conduct the Adelaide Symphony Orchestra. Even then it was for a studio recording for which I would receive the standard fee for an inexperienced local conductor of $60. The moguls in the ABC's Sydney headquarters probably couldn't understand how someone with my credentials could accept a position in Adelaide who had not been engaged by them. I agreed to conduct the studio recording as a visiting card as it were, but it still took a while before I was invited to conduct any other of the six symphony orchestras. Since that time, the musical life of Australia has developed fantastically and is now as sophisticated as anywhere in Europe or America.

For the 1976 Adelaide Festival we commissioned one-act operas from two Australian composers, George Dreyfus and Larry Sitsky, but they were as a bit of a shock for the staid Adelaide audiences and even for Don Dunstan the broad minded and highly intelligent Premier of South Australia. Larry had fused Chaucer's bawdy *The Miller's Tale* with Boccaccio's equally bawdy Decamaron and called the opera *Fiery Tales* but one reviewer wrote, *'It left me cold. The sight and sound of copulation and urination to atonal music left a lot to be desired'*. Another critic, reviewing *The Lamentable Reign of King Charles the Last* by George Drefus, wrote, *'For crass bad taste, bad humour and an overall adolescence it was unmatched in my experience'*. It was a far cry from the success of *Così fan tutte* and *The Turn of the Screw* the previous year and the good will that the company had been building up received a setback.

During my six years in Adelaide we gave Australian premières of Cavalli's *L'Ormindo*, Massenet's *Werther*, Puccini's *La Rondine*, Nicholas Maw's *One Man Show* and Monteverdi's *The Coronation of Poppea*, sung in

English in Raymond Leppard's realisation reduced to a string quartet, two harpsichords, organ and two trumpets (with his permission). *The success is largely due to the superb musical direction of Myer Fredman who has taught the orchestra, continuo players and singers to perform the idiosyncrasies of the 1642 score so that the musical flavour exactly matches the dramatic conventions of the period. He also managed to bring together one of the strongest casts heard here on the operatic stage.'* Justin moved to Sydney around this period so a new General Manager was appointed who gradually lifted the company out of its financial morass and guided it towards becoming a statutory body, The State Opera of South Australia. While Her Majesty's Theatre was being refurbished as our own theatre in 1976 we performed Cimarosa's *The Secret Marriage* in the University's Lecture Theatre which had a series of steps up from the auditorium to the stage. Suddenly in the middle of the Dress Rehearsal a troupe of fireman in burnished helmets and carrying their hatchets marched down the aisles, mounted the steps and disappeared into the set while we played on without batting an eye. Apparently the excessive heat of the stage lighting had activated the fire station's alarm bells. I was assured it wouldn't happen again, but sure enough on the opening night it certainly did! Another incident equally worthy of Berlioz's *Les Soirées de l'orchestre* was being invited to a seminar for musicologists about a completely forgotten eighteenth-century Neapolitan librettist. When I enquired about the music I was petulantly informed that they were only interested in the libretto!

I conducted many concerts and recordings with the Adelaide Symphony Orchestra ranging from light opera and musical comedy to Puccini's first opera *Le Villi*, which was produced by none other than John Culshaw, famous for his recording with Solti of the *Ring*. It would have been the first ever recording of *Le Villi* but by the time the ABC finally issued it in 1981, another had been released with an international cast. A tour with the ASO took me to the Northern Territory to Alice Springs and Darwin, but the road between Alice Springs and Darwin seemed endless so we stopped for refreshment at the only sign of habitation as far as the eye could see: a pub with one customer. After suitably quenching our thirst we continued for about another 200 miles when a very fast car overtook us and pulled up about 100 yards in front. The driver got out holding a rifle and waved us to stop, which we did of course and then he ordered us to put our hands on top of the car. I assumed that we were about to be robbed or worse when our driver and his companion – the compere for our concert (a local television celebrity) – simultaneously grabbed him, one by the throat and the other taking his rifle. The man had been the solitary customer in the pub who, having recognised our TV compere, blurted out in a broad Belfast accent, *'I'm an old Territorian and welcome you to God's own Country'*! The Darwin concert was in the open air so we had to rehearse in the blazing sun with the musicians facing in all directions (even mine) to avoid ruining their instruments. A year later I returned to Darwin, this time with June Bronhill as the soloist. The concert was also in the open air but at night, so the powerful arc lights attracted all kinds of weird and wonderful tropical insects and with every breath she swallowed a bucketful.

A more moving occasion was when the Italian communities around Adelaide organised a cultural festival which would have as its centrepiece Verdi's *Requiem*, and they asked me to be the conductor. As no Italian choir actually existed, my assistant rehearsed many small groups for months on end and then they all came together with me for the final rehearsals. Despite their very obvious lack of musical and vocal skills, performing Verdi and especially the *Requiem* was a highly charged experience for them. And when they discovered that I had been awarded a medal by the Italian Government, they began to address me respectfully as Maestro and even Commendatore. Another unusual occasion occurred when I conducted Rossini's *Petite Messe Solonelle* in the Cathedral during the 1980 Festival. About half way through the work I became aware that the choir and soloists were not focusing their attention on me but somewhere to my left. Bernard Levin described the event in the London *Times*, which was reprinted in his anthology

Silent Night: '*Half-way through, a lunatic lady left her seat and clambered onto the conductor's rostrum. The baton was in the hands of Myer Fredman, who kept his nerve magnificently, even when the intruder, having studied his technique, began to wave her arms about in a most commendable impersonation, though her beat was rather more in the misty style of Furtwängler than the crisper technique of Mr. Fredman. She was led away, gently.*'

The first time I conducted the Tasmania Symphony Orchestra I noticed a visitor's autograph book in the conductor's room and glancing through its pages I came across the name of Peter Ustinov who had just performed with the TSO on behalf of UNICEF: it read '*Thank you, Hobart von Karajan*'. On my next visit to Hobart the TSO asked me to include *The Campbell Town Waltzes* by a local nineteenth-century composer as we were scheduled to give a concert in his hometown during the orchestra's tour of the island. At the reception afterwards, the Mayor thanked us for performing the Waltzes and then went on proudly to tell us that '*Johann Strauss must have learnt an awful lot from our Mr. Henslowe*'. My third visit turned out to be even more of an adventure because the airlines were on strike so I was driven from Adelaide to Melbourne (an eight-hour journey) and then flew with a private airline in a small, single engine plane. Consequently it had to refuel on King Island in Bass Strait, well known as the Roaring Forties as it's one of the stormiest oceans in the Southern Hemisphere. After being buffeted about in the air for an hour or so we landed in Hobart where I was immediately driven to the rehearsal with both my mind and body still somewhere over Bass Strait.

During my six years in Adelaide, the company undertook three tours, the first being to Perth in Western Australia for its Festival with *Figaro* in the New Fortune Theatre with a string quartet and single woodwind instruments, which was perfectly appropriate for Mozart though the local purists thought otherwise. The last act especially was well suited to the open-air theatre for peacocks visibly and vocally joined the cast as the evening progressed. A year later, we took

Nicholas Maw's *One Man Show* to Sydney which was a success with the critics although not with the conservative opera-going public. In 1979 we took the company to Hobart where we performed Cimarosa's *The Secret Marriage* in the Theatre Royal; an ideal setting as the theatre was built in 1837 not long after the opera had been first performed. The local critic wrote, *'What Myer Fredman created would be accepted with respect in Vienna where the work had its first performance in 1792.'* I returned to Perth to conduct for an artist making her first tour of the Antipodes though her name was unfamiliar as it was to the majority of Australians. When we met for our piano rehearsal, I was taken aback by the majestic lady who walked through the door: it was Jessye Norman. At one point in Wagner's *Wesendonck Lieder*, Jessye asked me if I would encourage the orchestra to drown her – as if that was possible – and when she made her entrance on the platform for the performance, her 'presence' was electrifying. I hardly needed to conduct and allowed the orchestra to sense her supreme musicality and respond accordingly. Towards the end of the same year my wife and I stayed in a friend's apartment in London and, unknown to us, he had organised a surprise party in our honour. In walked Geoffrey Parsons, Peter Gellhorn, Richard Van Allan and the great lady herself, Jessye Norman.

In London I also met Sir Michael Tippett who was going to be present at our Australian première of his *Midsummer Marriage* at the next Adelaide Festival with Raymond Herincyx in the role of King Fisher and the remainder of the cast entirely Australian. Sir Michael came to our very bold venture but because of the numbers involved we had to rehearse in a large warehouse with no air-conditioning, so we all perspired profusely in a typical South Australian summer, though no one complained but worked with great enthusiasm on Sir Michael's opera. One London music critic described our production in glowing terms. *'Musically I have few quibbles about this presentation, Myer Fredman conducting the Adelaide Symphony Orchestra obtained rich textures, a lot of excellent playing from the principals (notably the first trumpet) and managed to pace the music well in relation to the stage action. The singers were never overwhelmed. Indeed, this*

Camera rehearsal for an ABC television programme with the Sydney Symphony Orchestra.

Rehearsing of Richard Strauss's *Vier Letzte Lieder* (Four Last Songs) with Elizabeth Söderström and The Sydney Symphony Orchestra, 29 September 1984.

cast of nearly all Australian soloists made light work of their difficulties and seemed to have taken the work to heart'. Sir Michael was equally pleased and while in Adelaide he conducted his *Fourth Symphony* with the ASO but I have to admit that the score mystified me.

In September 1978 Jani died. Chim, Spike Hughes' wife, wrote that Jani had only recently been to their house for dinner and suddenly said *'Myer is coming at Christmas so I have that to look forward to'*. Moran also wrote to me with the news and ended with a typical courteous observation, *'One automatically says "Poor old Jani" but I am not so sure we shouldn't say "Lucky old Jani" in the way his life surmounted so many difficulties with humour and elegance'.* Two years later it was my turn to write an obituary, this time for John Pritchard, in an Australian magazine devoted to opera, *'John was a very relaxed, gentle and charming man who had a disarming ability to beguile, whether in conversation or on the rostrum. With a very few succinct words couched in elegant phraseology he conveyed his intentions with the minimum of fuss or tension.'* Differences began to arise between the General Manager and myself and I thought of returning to England rather than renew my contract which, as it happened, was due for re-negotiation. Nevertheless I was rehearsing Britten's *Death in Venice* for its Australian première at the 1980 Adelaide Festival and it was like being back in Glyndebourne for Britten had composed the opera not only for Peter Pears but for an ensemble of soloists who, between them, perform many cameo roles. One was a young tenor, Glen Winslade, who was making his debut in the profession and now is a very successful international artist.

Not long after *Death in Venice* and the announcement in the Press that I would be leaving, I received a letter from someone who had been in the audience. *'One can count on one's fingers the number of truly great performances one hears and sees in one's life. And great it could not have been without superb musical direction based on fine perception of what is a particularly moving and personal statement to a unique degree.'* The anonymous letter continued, *'Sadly I have come to the conclusion that Australia goes for the meteor — the spectacular newcomer,* even if all ends in tears. I am not a great one for mayhem and martyrdom myself. The people who keep their heads down and go on doing their jobs without drawing publicity to themselves by various antics are really disregarded. I think it's because the arts here are top heavy. They do not have the solid base that comes from continuous and dedicated work, and that's partly why they are so often in trouble. Whatever the situation, I'm not alone in knowing and admiring what you have achieved. This is not flattery. I've been around too long and done too much to bother with that, but for those same two reasons I think praise should be given where praise is due, loud and clear.'* I had committed the cardinal sin for any Musical Director: failing to cultivate the Board because I was unable to play politics. As I was not going to renew my contract, my wife and I decided to return to England when it expired but without a permanent position or financial security, we would probably have to live in a bed-sitter (again) if needs be. In the following months I received an invitation from Opera North to conduct *The Magic Flute* which at least was a good omen.

I had still two engagements to fulfil, the first in Melbourne for Bach's B Minor Mass in which one of the soloists was Grant Dickson with whom I had worked on a number of occasions. He also taught singing at the Sydney Conservatorium and during a break in rehearsals I asked after Ronal Jackson, the Head of its Opera School. Grant's reply was that Ronal was due to retire and the position would soon be vacant *'That's an opportunity for you'*. Without stopping to think I said, *'Oh no, we've already set our plans in motion to return to England'*, but on the return flight to Adelaide I began to reconsider. The next day I phoned the Director of the Sydney Conservatorium who expressed interest in having someone of my calibre running the Opera School and suggested that I fly over to discuss the matter which I then did. Being a Public Service appointment the position had to be advertised and it was a nail biting few months while I waited, and even longer before it was confirmed: only one week before we were due to fly back to England.

My farewell to The State Opera was with *Onegin*, ironically the opera that Justin and I had planned for my debut six years earlier. A photo taken during rehearsals shows how haggard I had become from the stress of the preceding months. My self-confidence was boosted, however, by a letter from Sir Walter Crocker KBE who, before his retirement, had been an important diplomat and the Lieutenant Governor of South Australia: *'It is for others to discuss his technical competence. For the cultivated laity he stands for a combination of incontestable erudition in music, a fresh and spontaneous love for it, and the gift of transmitting his appreciation to his listeners. When he is conducting, whether an orchestra or a choir, he is always in control, his high standards are insisted upon, and this is done without either bossiness or pedantry.'* My final concert before my departure was in Hobart with Mattawilda Dobbs, who I remembered from my first year in Glyndebourne. While in Hobart I auditioned a talented all-round musician as my first repetiteur student in the Opera School in Sydney, which augured well for my new appointment.

After my departure successive Musical Directors brought about changes, which was only to be expected, but my policy of engaging young artists was gradually abandoned and in the course of time the company became merely a vehicle for the sure-fire standard repertoire with well-known singers. More recently the company has regained its former status with a repertoire that I would never have believed feasible. The State Opera has now become one of the major Richard Wagner Festivals around the world, with his music dramas including the complete Ring cycle. As a result, it has become a tourist attraction, thereby enhancing the economy of South Australia.

A new life begins

In the Conservatorium building my studio was below ground with only a small window through which I could just about see the feet of people strolling in the Botanical Gardens. Every so often, a health inspector would come to examine the damp and always came to the same decision that 'something had to be done about it', but after five years or so when nothing was, I removed the rotting carpet with its obnoxious smell and the health hazard. Now for the first time I had a tenured position, a regular income and superannuation but as I had never before worked in an educational establishment, institutional bureaucracy, in-fighting and an academic mentality was a very new experience. I treated the opera students as young professionals and instead of academic classes from 9 to 5 and opera production at night, we rehearsed during the day when young voices, minds and bodies are all at their freshest. For the major productions I chose operas that stretched their imaginations without straining their voices rather than the more popular operas as our audiences — such as they were — the 'populars' could see and hear down the road at the Sydney Opera House. The major productions ranged from *Poppea, Pelleas, Riders to the Sea* to *The Comedy on the Bridge* (Martinu) and *La clemenza di Tito* in which Ron Dowd willingly agreed to sing the title role. Unfortunately he had to cancel for personal reasons which was a pity as the students would have gained a great deal from working in close proximity with such a fine artist. Quite a number of Opera School students went on to make national and international careers and several of the repetiteur students joined the Australian Opera. One in particular — Simone Young — was allowed to conduct matinée performances of Gilbert & Sullivan but as no more conducting eventuated, she went to Europe, made a considerable name for herself as a conductor, and was then invited back to conduct for her alma mater. In due course, after further international success and returning to conduct a number of times, she became Music Director of Opera Australia but later resigned after considerable artistic differences with the General Manager and the Board of Directors. Simone Young is currently not only the Music Director but also the Intendant in Hamburg and is much sought after all over the world. Alongside my work in the Opera School I established a scholarship with a philanthropic organisation to study conducting with me privately, and a number of young conductors have since embarked on successful careers in Australia, Vienna, America and Europe.

In conference with Sir Charles Mackerras and Neil Flottmann, who won the Willem van Otterloo Scholarship to study conducting with me, August 1983.

Rehearsing the Sydney Symphony Orchestra in the Sydney Town Hall.

A *Cosi fan tutte* production rehearsal on the Glyndebourne stage, 1969. The conference was to discuss a cut in one of the Recitatives requested by Franc Enriquez, the producer. Standing are Jane Berbié, Despina; John Pritchard, Musical Director; Myer Fredman; and Jani Strasser, Head of Music Staff & Preparation. On the stage are Hanneke van Borke, Fiordiligi; Martin Isepp, Coach and Continuo player; Franco Enriquez, Producer; and Roger Brunyate, Assistant Producer.

I was also able to continue conducting with the five ABC orchestras and the Australian Opera (renamed Opera Australia). I conducted *The Apocalypse* by Eugene Goossens for the ABC's twenty-fifth anniversary but the score had to be completely re-copied for the occasion, a mammoth undertaking in itself. He had composed it on a scale to equal Mahler's *Symphony of a Thousand*, but as Sydney was unable to muster a large enough choir, many small suburban choirs were enlisted for the performance and for the studio recording to follow. In the week before the concert the ABC finally agreed not to record *The Apocalypse* in the studio as the choral weaknesses would be evident but to record the live performance. Consequently I had the Opera House Concert Hall and a very large orchestra at my disposal. I proposed *Job* by Vaughan-Williams as, at that time, the only available recording was Sir Adrian's mono recording from just after the Second World War. The performance of *The Apocalypse* was recorded and released on an in-house disc but the splendid recording of *Job* has never been commercially released. For the ABC's celebration I also conducted the première of Peter Sculthorpe's television opera *Quiros*, which was broadcast only once and never seen again for reasons unknown to me as Peter had been delighted with the music. The opera portrays the voyage of the Spanish captain Quiros who was determined to discover the Great South Land — Terra Australis — but the expedition failed and he descended into madness. One particular concert was very nostalgic, for I conducted the Sydney Symphony Orchestra in the *Vier Letzte Lieder* (Four Last Songs) by Richard Strauss for Elizabeth Söderström. Elizabeth had been the superb Octavian in *Der Rosenkavalier* during my first year at Glyndebourne in 1959 and conducted the backstage orchestra along with me with her arms under mine.

My time at the Conservatorium also covered the early years of the Sydney Piano Competition when I had to be ready with virtually all the major Romantic and Modern piano concerti of the past two hundred years. The finalists could only be chosen after the solo recitals had finished and, as a result, the list was narrowed down to three, but only on the Monday preceding the concert: Beethoven's *Emperor*, Tchaikovsky's No. 1 and the Brahms *D minor*. The finalists and I had private rehearsals followed by a run-through with the orchestra on the day of the live, televised broadcast from the Sydney Opera House. The pianist who had chosen the Brahms had seemed to me as if he might possibly win as he had shown great musicality and brilliance in the solo heats, but that proved not to be the case. Just before going on stage, he whispered that he hadn't expected to reach the finals so he had to learn the concerto in two days, and would I conduct it really slowly to give him time to remember what came next. Needless to say he didn't win but the pianist who did with the *Emperor* hasn't been heard of since! Every summer Opera Australia performs one of the operas in the company's current season in the opera air in Sydney's Domain; it is a free performance for the public. I conducted a number of them including *La Bohème* and a semi-staged performance of *Die Zauberflöte*. The singers had to perform behind my back with closed circuit television monitors but to make matters even more difficult, the Queen of the Night was suspended on a crane high above the shell housing the orchestra. It was visually most effective but precarious for us both, especially when the fireworks exploded all round her.

Guest appearances in South America took me to Montevideo and Buenos Aires and in the former I conducted two works by Peter Sculthorpe, *Mangrove* and *Port Essington*, to promote Australian music, along with the *Second Symphony* by Sibelius. In *Mangrove* Peter uses the term *fuori di passo* – literally, 'out of step' – where he wants the cello section not to play together but some a little in front of, and others a little behind the beat, like a shadow. This created something of a problem as orchestral musicians all over the world spend their entire working lives trying to play in time with each other. In Buenos Aries, the orchestra's rehearsal premises were on the top floor of a sky-scraper so every player and their instruments ascended by elevator and when it broke down (often), the musicians refused to rehearse because they wouldn't climb the stairs. As a result I conducted both Richard Strauss'

Don Juan and his *Till Eulenspiegel* (a managerial request) – works that require ample rehearsal – as well as an overture and a concerto, after only two rehearsals.

Ten years of trying hard to create an opera school on a professional footing with inadequate facilities was enough so I resigned from the Conservatorium but continued with many conducting engagements and Opera Australia appointed me one of their Artistic Associates. For the company I conducted a wide-ranging repertoire from *Eugene Onegin, Werther, La traviata,* to *Lucia di Lammermoor* and all of Mozart's major operas including a new one for me, *La clemenza di Tito*, and a revival of our Adelaide Festival production of *Death in Venice*. For Naxos records I recorded CD's of Britten and Delius in New Zealand where we were housed in a cavernous hall during a bitterly cold spell. While we rehearsed an enormous and noisy industrial heater was switched on to warm us but switched off before each "take" by which time we were frozen again. My conversation with Eric Fenby of many years previously about Delius not having a fixed tempo as each phrase grows out of the preceding one was invaluable even though the heater stopped and started.

Coming full circle

My wife and I began to think about turning to England once more, but after a quarter of a century it would be a case of 'out of sight is out of mind' and well-nigh impossible to regain a foothold in the profession. Then during a short holiday in Tasmania we decided to move to Hobart as the better option as the island's temperate climate and its culture have a great affinity with the England of our youth. The wheel has come full circle and I now enjoy life as well as music, having jettisoned most of the former music-making tensions. Young conductors from Tasmania and the mainland come for intensive study and my advice. I conduct the Hobart Chamber Orchestra with whom I am able to programme such challenging works as Elgar's *Introduction & Allegro for Strings,* Vaughan-Williams' *Tallis Fantasia* and the music of Peter Sculthorpe, the Tasmanian-born doyen of Australian composers with an international reputation. I am also the Principal Guest Conductor of the Tasmania Chorale and conduct them in major works by Bach, Handel, Mozart and Britten and last but by no means least have written four books including this one based on my experience in the profession.

My wife and I have often wondered whether coming to Australia had been the right decision but having a rare opportunity to establish an opera company and conduct many interesting projects might never have arisen if I had chosen to return to Brussels instead of accepting the Sydney invitation. Misquoting Shakespeare, some are born successful, some achieve success and some have success thrust upon them, but being neither a metro-gnome nor a maestro, I fit somewhere into the second category despite having never been an egocentric megalomaniac and unable to 'use my elbows' as Joan had advised. Whether the relative success I achieved was the result of family and social background, education or simply the measure of an innate talent it is impossible to analyse, but I was fortunate indeed to have mentors of the calibre of Joan Cross, Peter Gellhorn and of course, the indomitable Jani Strasser.

Postlude

Table of equivalent note values

English	Italian	American	German
Breve	Breve	Double whole-note	Doppeltakt-note
Semibreve	Semibreve	Whole-note	Ganz Taktnote
Minim	Minima or bianca (white)	Half-note	Halbenote

Crotchet	Semiminima or nera (black)	Quarter-note	Viertel
Quaver	Croma	Eighth-note	Achtel
Semiquaver	Semicroma	Sixteenth-note	Sechzehntel
Demisemiquaver	Biscroma	Thirtysecond-note	Zweiund-dreissigstel
Hemidemisemi-Quaver	Semibiscroma	Sixtyfourth-note	Vierund-Sechzigstel

English-speaking members of the concert-going public will hardly ever – if at all – come across the French note values, but unlike the English and Italian designations, the American and German equivalents are completely logical in that they clearly define their relative mathematical sub-divisions.

How fast is slow

Any tempo is dependent on a subjective approach to the meaning of the indication that the composer inscribes above the first bars of a work. For baroque musicians (before conductors became necessary), tempo indications and/or time signatures were sufficient to give the pulse that arose from a ratio of heavy and light stresses derived from a central axis of *Andante* at approximately 92 pulses to the minute. Slower tempi were indicated as *Andantino*, *Larghetto* and *Adagio*, and the quicker ones as *Allegretto* and *Allegro* with, at the extremes, *Grave*, *Lento*, and *Largo* on the one hand, *Presto*, *Prestissimo* on the other. There were occasional qualifying terms such as *Maestoso*, *Grazioso*, *Vivace*, and the adjectival *assai*. If there was no indication it was assumed that the smallest rhythmic pattern would be a sufficient indication while *Allegro* without a qualification would have been interpreted as what Handel designated *Allegro commodo*, or later composers, *Allegro Moderato*.

After Johann Maelzel invented the metronome in 1815, giving the mathematical equivalents of the Italian terms, it was believed that a solution had been found, but a metronomic beat should never be continuously maintained for, music like a river must ebb and flow. Tempo indications are in reality a guide to the conductor's instinct, as every phrase and tempo should have an imperceptible progression to and from its apex and cannot be precisely expressed either on paper or metronomically as it's *'what lies behind the notes'* to quote Mahler.

During the nineteenth century some indications were differently interpreted in different cultures because composers had only a passing knowledge of the Italian language, so one or two began to write tempo indications in their native tongue. Mahler, for instance, used both Italian and German and headed the fourth movement of his *Fifth Symphony*, *Adagietto*, and its tempo, *Sehr langsam* (very slow); the movement is worlds away from the lighter version of an *Adagio* as understood by in earlier era.

As tempo indications are often printed in programme notes or on the television screen, the following definitions which have been gleaned from many sources, may be of some help.

Adagio	Slowly, peacefully, smoothly, softly.
Adagietto	Diminutive of *Adagio*: not as slow as an *Adagio* but not as quick as an *Andante*.
Andante	At a walking pace; not necessarily slow or serious.
Andantino	The diminutive of *Andante*: a little faster than *Andante*.
Allegretto	The diminutive of *Allegro*: brisk or jolly at a speed between *Andante* and *Allegro*.
Allegro	Cheerful, bright, good humoured, lively.
Grave	Weighty, serious, solemn, momentous.
Largo	Broad, wide.
Larghetto	Diminutive of *Largo*: not as slow as a *Largo*.
Lento	Slowly
Moderato	At a moderate pulse.

Presto	Quick, swift, nimble.
Prestissimo	Faster than *Presto*.
Vivace	Brisk, lively, sprightly and faster than *Allegro*.

Some tempo qualifications

Assai	Rather, or even more so.
Con brio	With brilliance or animation.
Grazioso	Graciously.
Maestoso	With majesty.
Mosso	With movement.
Quasi	As if, or somewhat like.
Tempo Giusto	The right tempo as demanded by the smallest rhythmic unit.

Beethoven's indication for the Kyrie Elison in his Mass in C was *Andante con moto, assai vivace, quasi allegretto ma non troppo* which literally translated becomes 'At a walking pace, with movement, rather brisk, as if between Andante and Allegro, but not too much!' The second movement of Sibelius' *Third Symphony* has the slightly less confusing *'Andantino con moto, quasi allegretto'*, although one edition of the viola part even has it printed simply as *'Allegretto'*. The perception of a tempo as to what one might expect is often the result of the density or weight of sound rather than its actual speed. Sir Thomas Beecham conducted Wagner observing the composer's metronome marks but was accused of being too fast and therefore, superficial for the dyed in the wool Wagnerites. He had lightened the texture which gave an impression of being faster without it actually being so.

*D*ancing on the rostrum

Bolero	Spanish dance in triple time (3 beats) Ravel's Bolero being the most famous.

Contradanse	Virtually any (country) dance in which the dancers stand opposite each other. One of the three dances simultaneously played in Mozart's *Don Giovanni* (Finale of Act 1).
Fandango	Spanish dance possibly originating in South America. In triple or compound duple time (2 or 3 beats) increasing in speed throughout; the dance is usually accompanied by castanets. In the third act of *Le nozze di Figaro* Mozart used a Fandango which in fact isn't one but a Minuet which he had 'borrowed' from Gluck.
Gavotte	Of French origin from the Pays de Gap where people were known as Gavots. In simple quadruple time (2 beats) with each phrase starting on the 3rd beat.
Gigue	Of Anglo Saxon origin (Jig in Ireland) in fast triple time (3 beats). Apart from Bach's keyboard Gigues, an orchestral example is Debussy's orchestral *Images*.
Habanera	In a steady duple time originally from Havana sometimes called by its other name of Havanaise; it was very popular in Spain. The most famous is the Habanera in Bizet's *Carmen*. The first beat is always in a dotted rhythm.
Ländler	Viennese dance in 3/4 time which was the forerunner of the Viennes Waltz.
Mazurka	Polish dance named after the people who lived in Mazovia near Warsaw, in triple time with a dotted rhythm. The most famous are those for piano by Chopin.
Minuet	Menuet (French) and Minuetto (Italian) in triple time that began as a stately peasant dance though taken over by the aristocracy. Virtually all the symphonies of Haydn and Mozart include Minuets with contrasting Trios. Beethoven also composed

	Minuets but vastly increased the tempo and renamed the movement, Scherzo.
Pavan	Or Pavane. Originally from Padova (Padua) in Italy but was taken over by the French and Spanish courts. It was in a stately duple time. A number of French composers of the early twentieth century revived the Pavane, the most famous being by Ravel.
Polka	A dance from Bohemia in the early nineteenth century in quick duple time favoured by Smetana and Johann Strauss amongst many others.
Polonaise	Polish national dance in a simple triple time in a steady tempo suggesting a dignified procession. The first beat was often divided and accented. The most famous orchestral Polonaise occurs in Tchaikovsky's *Eugene Onegin*, which is often played as a concert item. The dance is also known as a *Polacca*.
Saltarello	Italian dance in a simple triple or compound duple time similar to the *Tarantalla*, the most famous being the last movement of Mendelssohn's *Italian Symphony*.
Sarabande	Probably Spanish in origin but popular throughout Europe. Shakespeare described it as *full of state and ancientry* because of its steady rhythm and tempo. It was usually in triple time and, like the *Pavane*, was revived in the late nineteenth century by French composers.
Seguidilla	Spanish dance similar to the bolero and usually sung and accompanied by castanets, the most famous being in Bizet's *Carmen*.
Sicilienne	Believed to be of a pagan Sicilian origin in a compound duple or quadruple time in a rocking rhythm and often in a minor key.

Tarantella   From Taranto in Italy and also possibly derived from the spider (Tarantula) whose bite is poisonous! In a very fast compound duple time having an affinity with the *perpetuum mobile*. The most famous are by Rossini and the Finale of Mendelssohn's *Italian Symphony* where it is printed as being a Saltarello.

Valse   Usually known by its Viennese title of Waltz which is in simple triple time and descended from the *Ländler*. It has a moderately stressed first beat and slightly unequal second and third beats. The waltz epitomises the Austrian elegance and luxury of the late nineteenth and early twentieth centuries. There are examples by Josef, Johann and Richard Strauss (no relation), Tchaikovsky, Lehar and countless others.

What's in a name

Philharmonic, Philharmonia, Symphony or Sinfonia are merely names to distinguish one large orchestra from another: similarly Chamber Orchestra and Sinfonietta are smaller counterparts. A Concerto for Orchestra is comparable to a Symphony but composed ostensibly to exhibit an orchestra's virtuosity.

What does . . . mean?

Absolute pitch   The instinctive recognition of a note without having to play it on an instrument. It is an inherent talent and cannot be learnt or developed. *See also* Relative pitch.

A Cappella   Originally meaning in the church style but

	now tending to mean without accompaniment.
Alla breve	Performed with two beats in the bar.
Alla turca	In the style of a Turkish 'Janissary' band; Mozart wrote a number of works *alla turca*.
Arco	Played with the bow as distinct from plucking the string. See *pizzicato*.
Aria	Air or a song in an opera, operetta or oratorio.
Arietta	A shorter or lighter version of an Aria. Mahler used the term as a title for the fourth movement in his *Fifth Symphony* which was used in the film *Death in Venice*.
Arpeggio	The notes of a chord when played very quickly and spread from bottom to top, or the reverse.
Avant-garde	Originally meant the advance guard of an army but now implies creators or performers who are 'way out' in front of their colleagues.
Ausgabe	German for an edition or a score. See also *Partitur*.
Band	Name for a brass or military music ensemble and occasionally used in a derogatory manner for an orchestra.
Bar numbers	Numbers printed in the score, in fives and/or tens or at the beginning of each line or page. Used as reference points when re-starting during a rehearsal. See also *Rehearsal letters*.
Baroque	Originally an architectural term meaning excessively ornate or extravagant.
Basset Horn	A member of the clarinet family which Mozart used, especially in his 'Masonic' works; Beethoven, Spohr, Mendelssohn and Richard Strauss all wrote for the instrument.
Cadence	Latin 'to fall', which came to mean the conclu-

	sion of a phrase or the chords that end a piece of music.
Cadenza	Extension of the word cadence meaning the moment, often near the end of a movement, where the soloist is at liberty to exhibit virtuosity. They were extemporised at one time but later composers began writing their own.
Cantabile	An extra singing or smooth (legato) quality.
Cantata	A short work for voices and orchestra usually of a religious nature.
Cantilena	Similar to Cantabile and implying a smooth lyrical quality.
Cembalo	The Italian equivalent of the German Clavier, Klavier or the harpsichord that filled out the figured bass of the continuo part.
Cassation	A form similar to a divertimento and usually for a small orchestra. Written in a 'light' style as distinct from a symphony and usually performed in the open air.
Chaconne	A work constructed on a repeated bass line while over it the music undergoes much variation. The line sometimes moves to the middle or top with the variations around it. See also *Passagalia*.
Chromatic	Literally meaning 'colour', indicating notes foreign to the diatonic key, i.e. the intervening semitones.
Circular breathing	Clarinetists and oboists sometimes employ circular breathing by filling their cheeks to hold in the air pressure so as to sustain the tone while breathing through the nose.
Clef	The sign at the beginning of each line of music indicating treble, alto, tenor or bass voice or instrument.

Coda	The terminating bars at the end of a work.
Coloratura	A highly decorated part usually for a singer. See also *Fiortura*.
Col legno	Literally with the wood: the string player uses the wood rather than the hair. The most famous example is the *Danse macabre* by Saint-Saëns to represent the rattling bones of the skeleton.
Comprimario	A singer of secondary roles in an opera usually of a comic character.
Concertante	A work having concerto-like elements as in a *Concerto Grosso* to differentiate the players from the rest of the orchestra; also known as Concertino.
Con sordino	Italian for 'with a mute'.
Continuo	The instrument that fills out the harmonies based on the figured bass but can also mean any plucked instrument fulfilling the same purpose or the actual player. See also *Cembalo*.
Corno	Italian for horn.
Counterpoint	Lines that interweave as distinct from harmony, i.e. music conceived vertically as chords.
Crook	The coil of tubing inserted in a brass instrument that was used to change its pitch enabling the musician to play in a variety of keys.
Da capo	Literally 'from the head', meaning to repeat from the beginning. 'From the top' is the modern colloquialism.
Diatonic	The eight notes of the major and minor scales.
Dirigent	German for conductor.
Divertimento	Literally a diversion. Similar to a symphony

Postlude

	but in a lighter style and often with more movements.
Divisi	The division of the string parts into separate lines each with different notes of the harmony.
Ensemble	Any number of players or singers performing together.
Embouchure	A French word meaning the way woodwind players shape their lips to produce the sound.
Enigmatic scale	Made up entirely of whole tones which Debussy exploited. Verdi's *Ave Maria* in his *Quatre pezzi sacre* is another example. It is more usually known as the whole time scale.
Fantasia	A 'Fancy' implied a freedom of form in the Tudor period unlike the structured form of the classical sonata or symphony. The form virtually disappeared apart from the keyboard Fantasias by Mozart and Beethoven. Its original meaning was revived by Vaughan-Williams for his *Fantasia on a theme by Thomas Tallis*.
Fermata	Italian for pause.
Figured Bass	The harmonic structure expressed in a numerical shorthand under the bass line of the continuo part.
Fiortura	An embellished line of a virtuoso nature. See also *Coloratura*.
Fugue	A composition entirely based on one subject treated contrapuntally in a number of parts including inversion and augmentation and on different degrees of the scale.
Gran Cassa	Italian for a Bass Drum.
Köchel	Ludwig Köchel was an Austrian music historian who catalogued the complete works of Mozart. Using his numbering helps to iden-

	tify the many works composed by Mozart in any one genre.
Measure	Synonym for bar.
Masque	A court entertainment of a theatrical nature involving singing, dancing, acting and poetry in praise of the monarchy or nobility with the action carried forward by the dance. It was the forerunner of opera.
Maestro	Italian for 'Master', literally meaning a teacher. In church music he was known as Il Maestro di Capella and in Germany, Kapellmeister. It has lost something of its original meaning and is often used indiscriminately.
Measure	Synonym for bar.
Melos	A Greek word meaning melody implying the underlying line of musical thought.
Metronome	Invented by Johann Maelzel in 1815 to establish a universal agreement for the speed for each tempo. Beethoven was the first composer to use it.
Modulation	The movement from one key to another.
Moll	German for minor key.
Motet	A work for choir, usually of a religious nature and without orchestra.
Octave	The span of eight notes of the diatonic scale (tone, tone, semitone, tone, tone, tone, semitone).
Obligato	An important accompanying part to that of the principal's solo.
Opera buffa	Comic opera originally from Naples portraying characters from the lower level of society and performed as an Intermezzo in the middle of an *opera seria*.

Opera seria	Serious opera portraying noble characters, usually kings or queens or mythological subjects.
Opus	Latin for 'work' to itemise a composer's compositions.
Oratorio	A work for voices (choir and/or soloists) and orchestra and performed on the concert platform, usually on a religious subject.
Orchestration	The use of orchestral instruments for their individual colours. Some composers conceive a work in orchestral terms right from its conception while others write it as if for the piano and then orchestrate it.
Ostinato	A short figure usually with a strong rhythm which is repeated for a considerable number of bars.
Overture	Originally it was the music that began a stage performance intended to create the mood of what was to follow but in the course of time overtures were written purely for concert performance.
Partitur	German for the printed score. See also *Ausgabe*.
Passacaglia	See *Chaconne*.
Pizzicato	Plucking the string as distinct from using the bow.
Ponticello	Literally 'on the bridge', meaning to play with the bow on the bridge thereby making a vague whistling sound.
Postlude	The termination of a piece as distinct from the *Prelude* (beginning), and *Interlude* (middle). The modern colloquialism is 'Play out'
Recitative	To 'recite' the text on pitch as opposed to singing it. A secco (dry) recitative implies with harpsichord accompaniment and

	Recitativo accompanimento implies orchestral accompaniment.
Rhapsody	A work usually in one movement and often a free fantasy form in a national, popular or folk idiom.
Rehearsal letters	Letters printed in the score as reference points when having to stop and start during a rehearsal. See also *Bar numbers*.
Relative pitch	The ability to recognise different keys without resource to an instrument. Relative pitch can be developed through practice. See also *Absolute pitch*.
Repetiteur	A pianist who coaches singers, plays for production rehearsals, acts as a prompter, and undertakes other duties in an opera company.
Ripieno	In baroque music the main orchestra as distinct from the soloists, i.e. the concertino.
Ritornello	The prelude or postlude in a vocal or instrumental work or passage. Also used to indicate the main body of the orchestra as distinct from the solo section in a concerto grosso.
Rondo	Literally 'to come around', the name given to a movement in which a passage continually comes around alternating with new material.
Rubato	Literally 'to rob', but the time has to be 'paid back' or it turns into a Rallentando. See *Rallentando*.
Scherzo	Italian for 'joke', implying music of a light-hearted or 'unbuttoned' (Beethoven's term) kind. He was supposed to have first used it as a replacement for the Minuet movement in a symphony but, in fact, Monteverdi and some baroque composers had preceded him.

Postlude

Score	The printed music for a vocal or instrumental ensemble.
Senza sordino	Without a mute, i.e. to take it off.
Sinfonia	A previous term for Overture and now sometimes used as a synonym for a chamber orchestra.
Sinfonietta	A small symphony both in character and size of ensemble, but Janácek's Sinfonietta is for large orchestra! It is also a synonym for various chamber-sized orchestras.
Sitzprobe	German meaning 'rehearsal while seated'. It specifically refers to the rehearsal in which the singers become accustomed to the orchestra after the production rehearsals with piano.
Sonata form	The constructional basis of the first and other movements of symphonies first composed by C. P. E. Bach and Haydn.
Sostenuto	An increased sustaining of a note or phrase.
Sostituto	An assistant conductor who stands in for the principal conductor.
Sotto voce	'Under the breath' but in instrumental music it implies a special hushed sound.
Stave	The five lines and four spaces that constitute the staff on which notes, rhythms and expression marks are written.
Symphony	Originally in three or four movements, but Romantic and later examples have been composed in any number ranging from one (Sibelius' *Seventh*) to five (Berlioz, Tchaikovsky and Mahler) or, very occasionally, more.
Symphonic Poem	A work that tells a story or event in symphonic terms and is a synonym for Tone Poem. Liszt, Richard Strauss and Sibelius as well as many

	other composers have excelled in this form. Elgar's *Falstaff* is really a symphonic poem but he preferred to call it a symphonic study.
Tam Tam	Gong.
Tone	Has three meanings: (1) the quality of sound, (2) American for a note, (3) an interval in a scale made up of two semi-tones.
Tone Poem	See *Symphonic Poem*.
Tone row	Name given to a composition technique using all twelve chromatic notes in the octave initiated by Arnold Schoenberg.
Transposition	Music written in one key but sounding in another, referring mainly to instruments like the clarinet and trumpet. An accompanist transposes a song when the printed key is too high or low for the singer.
Trio	Three players or singers but also the name of the middle section of a Minuet or Scherzo.
Tromba	Italian for trumpet.
Turkish music	Music played by Turkish military bands known as *Janissary* music during the time of the Ottoman Empire. Haydn and Mozart and even Beethoven were familiar with it and wrote various pieces in the Turkish style. Being ostensibly street music it was scored without strings but with extra woodwind and percussion.
Upbeat	The conductor's indication for the singers or orchestra to start; also known as the preparatory beat, it is the equivalent of an intake of breath.
Ur-text	The original score.
Vibrato	Vibration of a string or voice to increase its intensity. It came into existence in string

music with the invention of the chin rest which allowed the player to hold the instrument firmly leaving the left hand free to vibrate the string on the fingerboard. The term is often confused with *tremolo* which, if excessively used in singing, produces an ugly sound that ultimately can destroy the vocal chords.

Vocal Score   The reduction of a full orchestra score of an opera or oratorio for rehearsal purposes.

Vorspiel   German for Prelude.

Maestro — Conductor or Metro-Gnome?

Sources of Quotations

The Craft . . . PAGE 1 *The definition of a conductor* . . . London Musical Opinion, 1890.

PAGE 3 *The conductor of the modern orchestra* . . . Boston Herald, 1891.

PAGE 5 *His is the will* . . . Bruno Walter, *Of Music & Music Making.* W.W. Norton & Co. New York, 1957. Translated by Paul Hamburger.

PAGE 5 *There is a danger* . . . Bruno Walter, *Of Music & Music Making.* W.W. Norton & Co. New York, 1957. Translated by Paul Hamburger.

Hearing is . . . PAGE 7 *When you get lost* . . . Robin Ray, *Words & Music.* Methuen, 1984.

Baton . . . PAGE 13 *The orchestra of the London* . . . Louis Spohr: in *Composers on Music*, edited by Sam Morgenstern. Bonanza Books, MCMLVI.

Health PAGE 14 *Conducting an orchestra* . . . A. W. Sedgwick. Institute for Fitness & Research and Training Inc. North Adelaide. South Australia, 1987.

Five minutes . . . PAGE 16 *Conducting should not be* . . . Hermann Scherchen: *Handbook of Conducting* translated by M. D. Calvocoressi. Oxford University Press (Sixth Impression, 1949).

PAGE 17 *The left hand has nothing* . . . Richard Strauss. *Betrachtungen und Erinnerungen.* Zurich (*Recollections & Reflections*) Boosey & Hawkes Atlantis, 1949.

PAGE 18 *Our conductors are* . . . Richard Wagner. *On Conducting.* Translated by E. Dannreuther. William Reeves & Co, 1887.

Have Baton . . . PAGE 23 *One can be an excellent* . . . Hugo Wolf quoted in *Composers on Music*, edited by Sam Morgenstern. Bonanza Books, MCMLVI.

Sources of Quotations

	PAGE 23 *When you are a guest* . . . Interview with Mariss Janssons. *Sydney Morning Herald*, 1995.
Pre-rehearsal	PAGE 25 *Must hear the score* . . . Hermann Scherchen, *Handbook of Conducting*, translated by M. D. Calvocoressi. Oxford University Press (Sixth Impression) 1949.
	PAGE 25 *He approached the score* . . . Bruno Walter, *Of Music & Music Making*, W.W. Norton & Co. New York, 1957. Translated by Paul Hamburger.
Facing the . . .	PAGE 27 *Never allow your feelings* . . . Bruno Walter. *Of Music & Music Making*. Translated by Paul Hamburger. W.W. Norton & Co. New York 1957.
	PAGE 27 *You have to arrive* . . . Interview with Mariss Janssons. *Sydney Morning Herald*, 1995.
	PAGE 28 *Placing them all together* . . . Sir Adrian Boult, *Boult on Music*. Toccata Press, 1983.
	PAGE 29 *You should do your best* . . . Letter from Leopold Mozart to his son. Emily Anderson: *Letters of Mozart & his family*. Macmillan & Co, London 1938.
Applause	PAGE 32 *Criticism of the Arts* . . . Article by Fred Blanks on his retirement as music critic of the *Sydney Morning Herald*, 1996.
Metro-gnome	PAGE 33 *If Hans Richter* . . . Richard Langham Smith. *Debussy on Music*, 1977. Secker & Warburg, London.
	PAGE 33 *There is no definition of music* . . . Sergiu Celibidache speaking in a film by Jan Schmidt-Garre. Paris, 1991.
Metamorphosis	PAGE 41 *Certainly not lacking* . . . Review of the Vienna orchestra in Beethoven's lifetime. Clive Brown, *The Listener*.
	PAGE 42 *The scales fell from my eyes* . . . Richard Wagner. *On Conducting*. Translated by E. Dannreuther. William Reeves & Co, 1887.
	PAGE 42 *Conductors are more dangerous* . . . Berlioz. *Grande traité d'instrumentation et d'orchestration modernes*. (Treatise on Instrumentation). Translated by Theodore Front. Dover Publications. New York, 1948/1991.
	PAGE 43 *As there has been an advance* . . . Franz Liszt: quoted in *Composers on Music* edited by Sam Morgenstern. Bonanza Books, MCMLVI.

Crossroads

PAGE 43 He [*Wagner*] *was bent* . . . Felix Weingartner: *Weingartner on Music and Conducting*. Dover Publications Inc. New York, 1969. Translated by Ernest Newman

PAGE 44 *Conductors don't have* . . . Robin Ray, *Words & Music*. Methuen, 1984.

PAGE 45 *For considerable periods* . . . Anonymous.

PAGE 46 *I have been going* . . . Letter from Vincent Plush an Australian composer and writer on musical subjects to *Limelight*, February 2005.

Further Books of Interest

Berlioz, Hector: *Treatise on Instrumentation* (revised Richard Strauss), 1904. Translated by Theodore Front. Dover Publications, Inc. New York, 1991.

Boult, Sir Adrian: *Boult on Music*, Toccata Press, 1983.

Cooke, Deryck: *The Language of Music*. Oxford University Press, 1959.

Del Mar, Norman: *Conducting Beethoven: Volume 1, The Symphonies. Volume 2, Overtures, Concertos, Missa Solemnis; Conducting Brahms*. Clarendon Press/Oxford University Press, 1992/1993.

Del Mar, Norman: *Anatomy of the Orchestra*. University of California Press/Faber & Faber, 1983.

Fredman, Myer: *The Conductor's Domain*. Elkin Music Services, 1999.

Fredman, Myer: *From Idomeneo to Die Zauberflöte*. Sussex Academic Press, 2002.

Fredman, Myer: *The Drama of Opera: exotic and irrational entertainment*. Sussex Academic Press, 2003.

Heyworth, Peter: *Conversations with Klemperer*, 1973. Faber & Faber, London, 1985.

Geissmar, Berta: *The baton and the jackboot*. Columbus Books, 1988.

Hughes, Spike: *Glyndebourne*. Methuen & Co., 1965.

Lebrecht, Norman: *The Maestro Myth*. Simon & Schuster, London, 1991.

Malko, Nickolai: *The Conductor & his Baton*. William Hansen, Copenhagen, 1950.

Scherchen, Hermann: *Handbook of Conducting*. Translated by M. D. Calvocoressi. Oxford University Press.

Strauss, Richard: *Betrachtungen und Erinnerungen (Recollections & Reflections)*. Zurich. Boosey & Hawkes. Atlantis, 1949.

Wagner, Richard: *On Conducting*. Translated by Edward Dannreuther, 1869. William Reeves, 185 Fleet St. E.C. 1887.

Walter, Bruno: *Of Music and Music Making*. 1957. W.W. Norton & Co., New York. Translated by Paul Hamburger.

Index

Abbado, Claudio, xi
Abbott, Bud, 65
ABC (Australian Broadcasting Corporation), 82, 83, 92, 94
absolute pitch, 6, 11, 103
Adagietto, 99
Adagio, 98, 99
Adelaide Arts Festival, 76, 82, 84–5, 86–8
Adelaide Festival Theatre, 76, 78
Adelaide New Opera Company, 76, 77, 78–83
Adelaide Symphony Orchestra, 76, 78, 80, 82, 83, 86–8
Adeney, Richard, 44
The Adventures of Mr. Broucek (Janácek), 76
advertising, 44, 45
agents, 31, 33
Albert Herring (Britten), 50, 51
alla breve, 104
alla turca, 104
Allegretto, 98, 99
Allegro, 98, 99
Allegro commodo, 98
Allegro Moderato, 98
alto clef, 9
alto flute, 9
Alva, Luigi, 70
Amadeus (film), 44
Andante, 98, 99
Andantino, 98, 99
Animal Farm (Orwell), 2
Anna Bolena (Donizetti), 61, 63
antique cymbals, 10
anvils, 10
The Apocalypse (Goossens), 94

applause, 23, 32, 34–5
L'après-midi d'un faune (Debussy), 10, 48
arco, 104
aria, 32, 104
Ariadne auf Naxos (Hofmannsthal/Strauss), 34
arietta, 104
arpeggio, 104
Arts College, Dartington, 49
Aschkenazy, Vladimir, 19
assai, 98, 100
Association of British Orchestras, 15
Auber, Daniel-François-Esprit, *Fra Diavolo*, 65
audiences, 24, 32, 44
Augustine, Saint, 12
Ausgabe, 104
Australian Broadcasting Corporation (ABC), 82, 83, 92, 94
Australian Opera, 75, 76, 79, 91, 94
 see also Opera Australia
avant-garde, 104
Ave Maria (Verdi), 107

Bach, C. P. E., 111
Bach, Johann Sebastian, 45, 50, 97
 Gigues, 101
 Mass in B Minor, 89
ballet, 39
 applause, 32
Banchieri, Adriano, 80–1
band, 2, 104
bar numbers, 104
Barber, Samuel, 9
Barber of Seville (Rossini), 26, 58–9, 75, 76
Barbirolli, Sir John, 19, 69
Barenboim, Daniel, 19, 21

Index

baroque, 41, 98, 104
Bartók, Béla, 74
bass drum, 8, 10, 107
bass oboe, 11
basset horn, 104
bassoon, 8, 9, 10, 11
Bastien and Bastienne (Mozart), 49
Bax, Arnold
    First Symphony, 51–2, 69
    Second Symphony, 51–2, 69
    Third Symphony, 10
Bayreuth pit, 15
BBC Chorus, 49
BBC Northern Orchestra, 48
BBC Scottish Orchestra, 48
BBC television operas, 64
Beecham, Sir Thomas, xi, 7, 12, 19, 23, 62
    conducting of *L'après-midi d'un faune*, 48
    conducting of *Fennimore & Gerda*, 70
    conducting of Wagner, 100
    conducting of *Die Zauberflöte*, 57
    'lollipops', 24
    and London Philharmonic Orchestra, 44
Beethoven, Ludwig van, 19, 24, 48
    basset horn, 104
    Choral Symphony, 11, 42
    as conductor, 41–2
    Emperor, 95
    Fantasia, 107
    Fidelio, 60, 80
    First Symphony, 41
    first use of metronome, 108
    Fourth Piano Concerto, 61
    Liszt's views on conductors, 43
    Mass in C, 100
    Minuets, 101–2
    scherzo, 101–2, 110
    Second Symphony, 58
    Seventh Symphony, 19
    Turkish music, 112
bel canto, 40
bell-tree, 10
Bellini, Vincenzo, *I Puritani*, 20, 55–7, 64–5
Benjamin, Arthur, 69
    Overture to an Italian Comedy, 62

Berbié, Jane, 56
Berg, Alban, 60
Bergman, Ingrid, 3
Berkeley, Lennox, *Divertimento*, 65
Berlioz, Hector, xi, 23, 111
    on conducting, 42
    Liszt's views on conductors, 43
    Les Soirées de l'orchestre, 40, 47, 83
    Treatise on Instrumentation, 7, 42
    use of ophicleide, 10
Bernstein, Leonard, 46
Besch, Anthony, 79
Billy Budd (Britten), 11
Bing, Rudolf, 35
Bizet, Georges
    Carmen, 64, 72, 75, 101, 102
    Le Docteur Miracle, 52, 53, 79
    Opera Comique, 76
    use of saxophone, 11
Blades, Jimmy, 80
Blanks, Fred, 32
The Boatswain's Mate (Smythe), 49
Boccaccio, Giovanni, *Decameron*, 82
Boethius, 12
La Bohème (Puccini), 48, 63, 74–5, 95
Bois Epais (Lully), 48
bolero, 100
Bolero (Ravel), 100
Borke, Hanneke van, 56
Borodin, Alexander, 48
Boston Herald, 3–4
Boulez, Pierre, 12
Boult, Sir Adrian, 6, 28–9, 44, 48, 58, 73–4, 94
Bournemouth Symphony Orchestra, 52, 59
Brahms, Johannes, 6, 45
    Piano Concerto in D Minor, 95
    Symphony No. 2, 72
    Third Symphony, 23
brass instruments, 5, 8, 10
Brecht, Bertolt, *The Threepenny Opera*, 79
breve, 97
Brian, Havergal, 10, 66
British National Opera Company, 70

Index

Britten, Benjamin, 49, 96, 97
   Albert Herring, 50, 51
   Billy Budd, 11
   Death in Venice, 10, 88, 96
   Gloriana, 51
   Let's make an Opera, 50, 87
   Noyes Fludde, 50
   Owen Wingrave, 64
   percussion department, 10
   Peter Grimes, 10, 51
   The Rape of Lucretia, 51
   Spring Symphony, 10
   television operas, 64
   Turn of the Screw, 51, 79, 80, 82
   use of tuba, 10
Bronhill, June, 84
Bruch, Max, *Second Symphony*, 66
Bruckner, Anton, *Eighth Symphony*, 15
Brunyate, Roger, 56
Bruscantini, Sesto, 55

Caballé, Montserrat, 62
cadence, 104–5
cadenza, 105
La Calisto (Cavalli), 69
Camden Festival, 52, 53, 70–1
The Campbell Town Waltzes, 85
cantabile, 105
cantata, 105
cantilena, 105
cantors, 41
Caplat, Moran, 35, 75, 77, 78, 88
a cappella, 103–4
Carmen (Bizet), 64, 72, 75, 101, 102
cassation, 105
Cavalli, Francesco
   La Calisto, 69
   L'Ormindo, 67, 72, 82
Celibidache, Sergiu, 27, 33
cello, 8, 9, 29
cembalo, 105
La Cenerentola (Rossini), 55
Chabrier, Alexis Emmanuel, 24
chaconne, 105

Chamber Concerto for Violin, Piano and Wind (Berg), 60
chamber music, 12
Chaucer, Geoffrey, 82
The Chinese Symphony (van Dieren), 71, 73
choirs, 8, 18, 48, 49, 77
Chopin, Frédéric, 101
Choral Symphony (Beethoven), 11, 42
Christie, George, 59
Christie, John, 59, 65
chromatic, 105
Cimarosa, Domenico, *Il matrimonio segreto*, 61, 62, 79, 83, 86
cimbasso, 10
circular breathing, 105
clarinet, 8, 9
clef, 9, 105
Clements, John, 49
La clemenza di Tito (Mozart), 91, 96
coda, 105
col legno, 106
Coleridge-Taylor, Avril, 20
coloratura, 106
The Comedy on the Bridge (Martinu), 91
The Comedy of Errors (Slade), 52
composers, 30–1, 41
comprimario, 106
con brio, 100
con sordino, 106
concertante, 106
Concerto Grosso, 106, 110
conducting, defined, xi, 1
conductors
   and ballet, 39
   comments on, 1–6
   contracts, 22–3, 31
   emanation, xi, 2, 17, 20, 34, 64, 70
   emergence and development of, 41–4
   gestures, xi, 4, 6, 16–17, 18, 41
   health, 13–15
   hearing accuracy, 6–7
   knowledge of composition, 7
   knowledge of instruments, 9–12
   knowledge of scores, 3, 8–9, 21, 25, 26, 42

Index

mistakes, 7
and opera, 36–40
practical experience, 18–21
programme planning, 23–4
relations with agents, 31, 33
relations with composers, 30–1
relations with leaders, 29–30
relations with managers, 31, 33
relations with record producers, 31
relations with soloists, 4, 30
rostrum needs, 28
selection of, 21–2
sympathy for a work, 25
talk during rehearsals, 4, 6
teaching of, 16
travel issues, 22–3
use of baton, 12–13
women as, xi, 20–1
working area, 17
see also rehearsals
continuo, 106
continuo players, 41
contra bassoon, 9, 10, 11
contradanse, 100–1
Cooper, Robert, 80
cor anglais, 9
cornet, 8
corno, 106
The Coronation of Poppea (Monteverdi), 58, 82–3, 91
Così fan tutte (Mozart), xi, 50, 53, 56, 58, 68, 69–70, 79, 80, 82
Costello, Lou, 65
counterpoint, 7, 47, 106
court dances, 39
Covent Garden, 51, 79, 81
Covent Garden Orchestra, 80
Cox, John, 76
Craig, Douglas, 53–4
crescendo, 17
criticism, 32–3
Crocker, Sir Walter, 90
Cromwell, Oliver, 65
crook, 8, 106
Cross, Joan, 49–51, 97

crotales, 10
crotchet, 20, 98
Culshaw, John, 83
Curzon, Clifford, 61
cymbals, 8, 10
Czech Philharmonic Orchestra, 80

da capo, 106
dance, 39, 100–3
A Dance Rhapsody (Delius), 11
Danse macabre (Saint-Saëns), 106
Davis, Sir Colin, 19, 57
De Walden Institute, 50
Death in Venice (Britten), 10, 88, 96
Death in Venice (film), 104
Debussy, Claude, 23, 33
  L'après-midi d'un faune, 10, 48
  enigmatic scale, 107
  Gigues, 11
  harp-pedalling notation, 11
  Images, 101
  and oboe d'amore, 11
  Opera Comique, 76
  Pelléas et Mélisande, 54, 58, 91
  and saxophone, 11
Decameron (Boccaccio), 82
Decca, 51
Delibes, Léo, 24
Delius, Frederick, 23, 96
  A Dance Rhapsody, 11
  Eventyr, 11
  Fennimore & Gerda, 70–1
  Lyrita recordings, 62, 69
  Requiem, 11
  Russell's television programmes, 69
  Song of the High Hills, 11
  The Walk to the Paradise Garden, 62
demisemiquavers, 9, 10, 98
Dempsey, Gregory, 87
detaché, 9
Dialogues des Carmélites (Poulenc), 10
The Diary of a Man who Disappeared (Janáček), 81
diatonic, 106
Dickson, Grant, 89
diminuendo, 17

Index

Dirigent, 106
discipline, 3–4, 5
divertimento, 106
Divertimento (Berkeley), 65
divisi, 107
Dobbs, Mattawilda, 90
Le Docteur Miracle (Bizet), 52, 53, 79
Don Giovanni (Mozart), 16, 55, 59, 60, 67, 74, 101
Don Juan (Strauss), 16–17, 95–6
Don Quixote, (Strauss), 11
Donizetti, Gaetano, 66
   Anna Bolena, 61, 63
   L'elisir d'amore, 58, 67
   Lucia di Lammermoor, 96
double bass, 8, 9
Dowd, Ron, 80, 81, 91
Dreyfus, George, *Lamentable Reign of King Charles the Last*, 82
Dunstan, Don, 82
Dvořák, Antonin, 24
   Eighth Symphony, 14
   First Symphony, 66

Edinburgh Festival Choir, 77
Edmunds, Thomas, 87
Eighth Symphony (Bruckner), 15
Eighth Symphony (Dvořák), 14
Einem, Gottfried von, *The Visit of the Old Lady*, 77
Elder Conservatorium, 79
Elgar, Sir Edward, 24
   Falstaff, 111–12
   In the South, 23
   Introduction & Allegro for Strings, 97
   Lux Christ, 73
   Pomp Circumstance March No. 2, 77
   Russell's television programmes, 69
   Second Symphony, 23, 35
   Violin Concerto, 24
L'elisir d'amore (Donizetti), 58, 67
emanation, xi, 2, 17, 20, 34, 64, 70
embouchure, 107
Emperor (Beethoven), 95
enigmatic scale, 107

Enriquez, Franco, 56
ensemble, 107
Die Entführung aus dem Serail (Mozart), 74
Eugene Onegin (Tchaikovsky), 66, 68, 69, 79, 89–90, 96, 102
euphonium, 11
Evans, Edith, 50
Evans, Geraint, 70
Eventyr (Delius), 11

Falstaff (Elgar), 111–12
Falstaff (Verdi), 20, 55
fandango, 101
fantasia, 107
Fantasia on a theme by Thomas Tallis (Vaughan-Williams), 97, 107
Fenby, Eric, 70–1, 96
Fennimore & Gerda (Delius), 70–1
fermata, 107
Fidelio (Beethoven), 60, 80
Fiery Tales (Sitsky), 82
Fifth Symphony (Mahler), 99, 104
Fifth Symphony (Sibelius), 61
figured bass, 7, 47, 107
fiortura, 107
First Symphony (Bax), 51–2, 69
First Symphony (Beethoven), 41
First Symphony (Dvořák), 66
flautato, 9
Flotow, Friedrich, *Martha*, 51
Flottmann, Neil, 93
flute, 8, 9, 11
folk dances, 39
Four Last Songs (Strauss), 92, 94
Fourth Piano Concerto (Beethoven), 61
Fourth Symphony (Tippett), 88
Fourth Symphony (Vaughan-Williams), 65
Fra Diavolo (Auber), 65
Fredman, Jeanne, 54, 66, 72, 76, 77, 97
French horn, 8–9
fugue, 7, 107
fuori di passo, 95
Furtwängler, Wilhelm, xi, 16

Gal, Erna, 54

Index

Gavazzeni, Gianandrea, 63
gavotte, 101
Gellhorn, Peter, 50, 52, 53, 54, 58, 86, 97
General Manager, 33, 35, 36, 44
Gershwin, George, 3
Gershwin, Ira, 3
gestures, xi, 4, 6, 16–17, 18, 41
gigue, 101
Gigues (Bach), 101
Gigues (Debussy), 11
Gilbert, Sir William, 48, 91
Giulini, Carlo Maria, 58
Glennie, Evelyn, 15
Gloriana (Britten), 51
Gluck, Christoph Wilibald, 101
Glyndebourne, 53–7, 58–60, 81
    1959 season, 53–4
    1960 season, 55–7
    1963 season, 60
    1965 season, 61–4
    1968 season, 66
    1970 season, 69
    Fredman joins (1959), 53–4
    Fredman leaves, 77–8
    General Managers, 35
    understudies policy, 58
Glyndebourne Chorus, 58–9, 60, 64
Glyndebourne (Hughes), 78
Glyndebourne Touring Opera, 58, 65, 66–8, 75, 77, 78, 81
Goossens, Eugene, *The Apocalypse*, 94
Die Götterdämmerung (Wagner), 45
Gounod, Charles Françoise, 76
Gran Cassa (bass drum), 8, 10, 107
Grant, Pauline, 77–8
Grave, 98, 99
grazioso, 98, 100
Group 8, 52
Groves, Charles, 52–3
Gruenberg, Peter, 79–80
Gui, Vittoria, 55, 59, 61, 62
Gurner, Ruth, 87

habanera, 101
Habeneck, François-Antoine, 42

Hamburg State Opera, 75
Hamburger, Paul, 53
Hamlet (Tchaikovsky), 23
Handbook of Conducting (Scherchen), 16
Handel, George Frederick, 23, 97, 98
    Messiah, 48
Hansel and Gretel (Humperdinck), 75–6
harmonics, 9
harmony, 7
harp, 8, 28
harp-pedalling notation, 11
Haydn, Franz Joseph, 101, 111, 112
Head of Music Staff, 36
hearing loss, 15
Ein Heldenleben (Strauss), 11
Helpmann, Robert, 81
hemidemisemiquavers, 98
Hempton, Keith, 87
Henslowe, Francis Hartwell, 85
Her Majesty's Theatre, Adelaide, 80, 83
Herincyx, Raymond, 86, 87
Hobart Chamber Orchestra, 96–7
Hofmannsthal, Hugo von, 34
Holst, Gustav, 45
    Savitri, 49
Holst, Imogen, 20, 49
Honegger, Arthur, *Jeanne d'Arc au Bûcher*, 3
horns, 8, 9–10, 28
Hughes, Chim, 88
Hughes, Spike, 60, 63, 73, 78, 88
Humouresques (Sibelius), 66
Humperdinck, Engelbert, *Hansel and Gretel*, 75–6

I Puritani (Bellini), 20, 55–7, 64–5
Idomeneo (Mozart), 53
Images (Debussy), 101
In the South (Elgar), 23
L'incoronazione di Poppea (Monteverdi), 58, 82–3, 91
instruments, 8–11, 28
Introduction & Allegro for Strings (Elgar), 97
Isepp, Martin, 53, 56, 64
Italian Symphony (Mendelssohn), 102, 103
Itter, Mr., 62, 69

Index

Jackson, Ronal, 89
Jacobs, Arthur, 52
Jaeger, A.J., 77
Janácek, Leos, 23
   The Adventures of Mr. Broucek, 76
   The Diary of a Man who Disappeared, 81
   Sinfonietta, 111
Janissary music, 112
Janssons, Mariss, 23, 27
Jarred, Mary, 81
jazz music, 41
Jeanne d'Arc au Bûcher (Honegger), 3
Job (Vaughan-Williams), 94
Johnson, Dr. Samuel, 35
Joyce, Eileen, 50

Keeping up Appearances, 52
Kempe, Rudolf, 5
Kessler, Susan, 87
Klemperer, Otto, xi, 58, 69–70
Köchel, Ludwig, 107
Koussevitzky, Serge, 19
Krips, Henry, 81
Krips, Josef, 81

Lambert, Constant, *Music Ho!*, 71
Lamentable Reign of King Charles the Last (Dreyfus), 82
The Land of Smiles (Lehar), 81
Ländler, 101, 103
Larghetto, 98, 99
Largo, 98, 99
legato, 17
Legge, Walter, 58
Lehar, Franz
   The Land of Smiles, 81
   waltzes, 103
Lento, 98, 99
Leppard, Raymond, 67, 69, 83
Let's make an Opera (Britten), 50, 87
Levin, Bernard, 84–5
'light' music, 24
Liszt, Franz, 42–3, 111
Liverpool Philharmonic, 60
The Lodger (Jack the Ripper) (Tate), 52

'lollipops', 24
London Philharmonic Orchestra, 44, 52, 69
London Philharmonic Society, 13
louré, 9
Lucia di Lammermoor (Donizetti), 96
Ludwig, Leopold, 54
Luisa Miller (Verdi), 68
Lully, Giovanni Battista, 12, 48
Lux Christ (Elgar), 73
Lyrita Record Editions, 51–2, 69

Maazel, Lorin, 7, 19
Macbeth (Verdi), 57, 67
Macdonnell, Justin, 76, 77, 79, 83, 89
Mackerras, Sir Charles, xi, 2, 19, 23, 64, 79, 93
Madame Butterfly (Puccini), 15, 37, 72
Maelzel, Johann, 98, 108
maestoso, 98, 100
Maestro, xi, 33–5, 108
The Magic Flute (Mozart), 20, 25, 55, 57, 63–4, 67, 69, 75, 89, 95
Mahler, Gustav, 14, 45, 70, 111
   Fifth Symphony, 99, 104
   rehearsals, 27
   Symphony of a Thousand, 94
   tempo, 99
   Walter on, 25
mallet, 10
Malmö Symphony Orchestra, 65–6
managers, 31, 33
   see also General Manager
Mangrove (Sculthorpe), 95
Mariner, Sir Neville, 19
marketing, 46
The Marriage of Figaro (Mozart), 58, 60, 62–3, 85, 101
martellato, 9
Martha (Flotow), 51
Martinu, Bohuslav, *The Comedy on the Bridge*, 91
masque, 39, 108
Mass in B Minor (Bach), 89
Mass in C (Beethoven), 100

Index

Massenet, Jules, 24
   Opera Comique, 76
   Werther, 67, 82, 96
Massine, Leonide, 39
Il matrimonio segreto (Cimarosa), 61, 62, 79, 83, 86
Matters, Arnold, 81
Maw, Nicholas, *One Man Show*, 52, 82, 86
mazurka, 101
measure, 108
Mehta, Zubin, 61
melos, 108
Mendelssohn, Felix
   basset horn, 104
   Italian Symphony, 102, 103
   use of ophicleide, 10
Messiah (Handel), 48
metronome, 98–9, 108
Metropolitan Opera, New York, 35
Midsummer Marriage (Tippett), 86–8
Milhaud, Darius
   Le Pauvre Matelot, 52
   use of saxophone, 11
Miller, Kevin, 81
The Miller's Tale (Chaucer), 82
minim, 97
Minton, Yvonne, 52, 70
minuet, 39, 101–2
Moderato, 99
modulation, 108
moll, 108
Monitor, 57–8
Monnaie Theatre, Brussels, 72, 75
Monteverdi, Claudio
   The Coronation of Poppea, 58, 82–3, 91
   scherzo, 110
Montgomery, Kenneth, 67
mosso, 100
motet, 108
Mozart, Leopold, 29
Mozart, Wolfgang Amadeus, 19, 23, 30, 45, 77, 97
   alla turca, 104
   basset horn, 104
   Bastien and Bastienne, 49

La clemenza di Tito, 91, 96
coperto, 10
Così fan tutte, xi, 50, 53, 56, 58, 68, 69–70, 79, 80, 82
Don Giovanni, 16, 55, 59, 60, 67, 74, 101
Die Entführung aus dem Serail, 74
Fantasia, 107
Idomeneo, 53
Köchel catalogue, 107
The Marriage of Figaro, 58, 60, 62–3, 85, 101
Minuets, 101
opera rehearsals, 38
Requiem, 59
Turkish music, 112
Die Zauberflöte, 20, 25, 55, 57, 63–4, 67, 69, 75, 89, 95
Music Ho! (Lambert), 71
Musica Viva series, 60–1
Musical Opinion, 1
Musicians Union, 1, 44

Naxos records, 96
Neel, Boyd, 65
New Fortune Theatre, Perth, 85
new music, 24
New Philharmonia Orchestra, 58
Nikisch, Artur, 16
Ninth (Choral) Symphony (Beethoven), 11, 42
Norman, Jessye, 86
Norrington, Roger, 52
Northern Sinfonia, 67
Norwegian Opera, 65
note values, 97–8
Noyes Fludde (Britten), 50
Le nozze di Figaro (Mozart), 58, 60, 62–3, 85, 101

obligato, 108
oboe, 8, 9
oboe d'amore, 11
octave, 108
Oedipus Rex (Stravinsky), 80
Of Music and Music Making (Walter), 5
Offenbach, Jacques, *Tales of Hoffmann*, 77

Index

One Man Show (Maw), 52, 82, 86
O'Neill, Dennis, 79
opera, 35–40
    applause, 32
    commercialisation, 45
    conductor's use of hands, 17
    and future generations, 46
    General Manager, 33, 35, 36
    Head of Music Staff, 36
    Music Director, 36–7
    orchestral pits, 39–40
    orchestras, 36–9
    production of, 37–9
    rehearsals, 38–9
    repetiteurs, 20, 38
    singers, 37–40
Opera Australia, 57, 94, 95, 96
    see also Australian Opera
opera buffa, 108
Opera Comique, 76
Opera North, 89
Opera School, 49, 50, 51
opera seria, 108–9
ophicleide, 10
opus, 109
oratario, 109
orchestras
    apprentice schemes, 19
    commercialisation, 44–5
    discipline, 3–4, 5
    and future generations, 46–7
    opera, 36–9
    role of leader, 29–30
    role of soloists, 4, 8, 30
    seating, 4, 5, 28–9
    Viennese, 41–2
    see also rehearsals
orchestras, amateur, 18
orchestras, student, 18
orchestration, 7, 109
L'Ormindo (Cavalli), 67, 72, 82
ORTF, 75
Orwell, George, 2
ostinato, 109
Otello (Rossini), 77

overture, 109
Overture to an Italian Comedy (Benjamin), 62
Owen Wingrave (Britten), 64

Park Lane Opera Group, 52
Parsons, Geoffrey, 53, 59, 86
Partitur, 109
passacaglia, 109
Le Pauvre Matelot (Milhaud), 52
pavan, 102
Pavillon dan l'air, 10
Pears, Peter, 88
Pelléas et Mélisande (Debussy), 54, 58, 91
percussion instruments, 8, 10–11, 28
Perth Festival, 85
Peter Grimes (Britten), 10, 51
Petite Messe Solonelle (Rossini), 84–5
Petrouchka (Stravinsky), 24
Philharmonia Orchestra, 69–70
Piano Concerto in D Minor (Brahms), 95
Piano Concerto No. 1 (Tchaikovsky), 95
Piatigorsky, Gregor, 34
piccolo, 9, 11
La Pietra del Paragone (Rossini), 52
pizzicato, 109
polka, 39, 102
polonaise, 102
Pomp Circumstance March No. 2 (Elgar), 77
ponticello, 109
Popp, Lucia, 70
Port Essington (Sculthorpe), 95
portato, 9
postlude, 109
Poulenc, Francis, *Dialogues des Carmélites*
    (Poulenc), 10
Prestissimo, 98, 100
Presto, 98, 100
Prince Regent Pavilion, Brighton, 76
Pritchard, John, 56, 58, 60–1, 69, 71, 88
Prokofiev, Serge, 9
Puccini, Giacomo, 23
    La Bohème, 48, 63, 74–5, 95
    Madame Butterfly, 15, 37, 72
    La Rondine, 73, 82
    Turandot, 15

Index

Le Villi, 83
pulse, 98

quasi, 100
Quatre pezzi sacre (Verdi), 107
quavers, 20, 98
Quiros (Sculthorpe), 94

The Rake's Progress (Stravinsky), 81
The Rape of Lucretia (Britten), 51
Ravel, Maurice
   Bolero, 100
   harp-pedalling notation, 11
   Pavane, 102
recitative, 109–10
record producers, 31
recording contracts, 22
Redgrave, Sir Michael, 67
rehearsal letters, 110
rehearsals, 4–5, 20, 24–9
   conditions, 27–8
   first encounter, 26–7
   opera, 38–9
   pre-rehearsal, 24–6
   psychology of, 4, 27
   role of composers, 30–1
   role of leader, 29–30
   role of soloists, 4, 30
   talk during, 4, 6
relative pitch, 110
repetiteurs, 12, 20, 36, 38, 39, 53, 110
Requiem (Delius), 11
Requiem (Mozart), 59
Requiem (Verdi), 84
rhapsody, 110
rhythm, 20, 43, 47
Richardson, Marilyn, 87
Richter, Hans, 33
Riders to the Sea (Vaughan-Williams), 91
Rigoletto (Verdi), 51, 72
Rimsky Korsakov, Nikolai Andreievich, xi
Der Ring des Nibelungen (Wagner), 83, 90
ripieno, 110
ritornello, 110
La Rondine (Puccini), 73, 82

rondo, 110
Der Rosenkavalier (Strauss), 20, 53, 54, 55, 94
Rossini, Gioachino Antonio, 20
   Barber of Seville, 26, 58–9, 75, 76
   La Cenerentola, 55
   Otello, 77
   Petite Messe Solonelle, 84–5
   La Pietra del Paragone, 52
   tarantella, 103
   Il turco in Italia, 69
Routledge, Patricia, 52
Roux, Michel, 62
Royal Academy of Music, 49
Royal Festival Hall, 51, 61, 62
Royal Philharmonic Orchestra, 62, 72
rubato, 110
Rubinstein, Artur, 48
Russell, Ken, 69
Rutherford, Margaret, 50

Sadlers Wells, 51, 80, 81
St. Pancras Festival, 52
Saint-Saëns, Camille, 11, 24
   Danse macabre, 106
Salad Days (Slade), 52
saltarello, 102, 103
San Francisco Opera, 80
sandpaper, 10
sarabande, 102
sarrusophone, 11
Savitri (Holst), 49
saxophone, 11
Schallrichter auf, 10
Scherchen, Hermann, 16, 25
scherzo, 102, 110
Schikaneder, Emanuel, 25, 63
Schindler, Anton, 41–2
Schoenberg, Arnold, 112
Schubert, Franz Peter, *Unfinished Symphony*, 23
scores, 110
   conductor's knowledge of, 3, 8–9, 21, 25, 26, 42
   layout, 8–9
Sculthorpe, Peter, 97
   Mangrove, 95

Index

Sculthorpe, Peter *(continued)*
    Port Essington, 95
    Quiros, 94
seating, 4, 5, 28–9
Second Symphony (Bax), 51–2, 69
Second Symphony (Beethoven), 58
Second Symphony (Bruch), 66
Second Symphony (Elgar), 23, 35
Second Symphony (Sibelius), 59, 95
The Secret Marriage (Cimarosa), 61, 62, 79, 83, 86
seguidilla, 102
Sehr langsam, 99
semibreve, 97
semiquavers, 98
senza sordino, 111
Serenades (Sibelius), 66
Seventh Symphony (Beethoven), 19
Seventh Symphony (Sibelius), 111
Shakespeare, William, 97, 102
Sharp, Cecil, 81
Shelley, Percy Bysshe, 35
Shirley, George, 63
Shostakovich, Dmitri, 14
Sibelius, Jan, 23, 24
    Fifth Symphony, 61
    Humouresques, 66
    Second Symphony, 59, 95
    Serenades, 66
    Seventh Symphony, 111
    symphonic poem, 111
    Tapiola, 11
    Third Symphony, 100
    Violin Concerto, 65
sicilienne, 102
side drum, 8
Siegfried Idyll (Wagner), 30
Silent Night (Levin), 84–5
Simpson, Robert, 66
sinfonia, 111
Sinfonia (Still), 61, 62
sinfonietta, 111
Sinfonietta (Janáček), 111
singers, 8, 20
    intake of breath, 18, 79

opera, 36–40, 58
    Wagner on, 18
    see also choirs
Sitsky, Larry, *Fiery Tales*, 82
Sitwell, Edith, 50
sitzprobe, 38, 111
Slade, Julian, 52
Smetana, Bedrich, 102
Smith, Dick, 80
Smyth, Dame Ethel, 20, 49
snare drums, 10
Söderström, Elisabeth, 54, 92, 94
Les Soirées de l'orchestre (Berlioz), 40, 47, 83
The Soldier's Tale (Stravinsky), 79
soloists, 4, 8, 30
Solti, Sir Georg, 83
sonata form, 111
Song of the High Hills (Delius), 11
soprano clef, 9
sostenuto, 111
sostituto, 111
sotto voce, 111
Souzay, Gérard, 62
spiccato, 9
Spohr, Louis, 13, 104
Spring Symphony (Britten), 10
staccato, 17
Stanford, Sir Charles, 7, 34
State Opera of South Australia, 83–90, 87
stave, 111
Steele, Anthony, 76, 77
Still, Robert, 69
    Sinfonia, 61, 62
    Third Symphony, 51
Strasser, Jani, 53, 54–5, 56, 57–8, 60, 69, 77, 97
    and Australian Opera, 76
    death of, 88
    retirement from Glyndebourne, 71
    Die Zauberflöte, 63–4
Strauss, Franz, 26
Strauss, Johann, 102, 103
Strauss, Josef, 103
Strauss, Richard, 23
    Ariadne auf Naxos, 34

Index

basset horn, 104
Don Juan, 16–17, 95–6
Don Quixote, 11
Ein Heldenleben, 11
euphonium, 11
perspiration, 14
Der Rosenkavalier, 20, 53, 54, 55, 94
symphonic poem, 111
Till Eulenspiegel, 95–6
Treatise on Instrumentation, 7
use of eyebrows, 16
use of left hand, 17
Vier Letzte Lieder, 92, 94
violins, 11
waltzes, 103
Stravinsky, Igor Fedorovich
  Oedipus Rex, 80
  Petrouchka, 24
  The Rake's Progress, 81
  The Soldier's Tale, 79
stress, 14
string instruments, 8, 9, 28, 41
Sullivan, Sir Arthur, 23, 48, 91
Sun Aria competition, 57
The Sunday Times, 52
Sutherland, Dame Joan, 57, 59
Sydney Conservatorium, 89, 90–6
Sydney Morning Herald, 32
Sydney Opera House, 15, 75, 91, 95
Sydney Piano Competition, 94–5
Sydney Symphony Orchestra, 92, 93, 94
symphonic poem, 111–12
symphony, 111
Symphony No. 2 (Brahms), 72
Symphony of a Thousand (Mahler), 94

Tales of Hoffmann (Offenbach), 77
Tallis Fantasia (Vaughan-Williams), 97, 107
tam tam, 112
Tancibudek, Jiri, 80
Tannhäuser (Wagner), 66
Tapiola (Sibelius), 11
tarantella, 102–3
Tasmania Chorale, 97
Tasmania Symphony Orchestra, 85

Tate, Phillis, 52
Tausky, Vilem, 50
Tavener, John, *The Whale*, 64
Tchaikovsky, Piotr Ilyich, 19, 111
  Eugene Onegin, 66, 68, 69, 79, 89–90, 96, 102
  Hamlet, 23
  Piano Concerto No. 1, 95
  waltzes, 103
tempo, 2, 17, 34, 36, 98–100
  Beethoven Minuets, 101–2
  and Delius, 96
  jazz music, 41
  and Klemperer, 70
  and metronome, 98–9, 108
  Polonaise, 102
  sarabande, 102
  Wagner on Habeneck, 42
  Wagner on, 18
tempo giusto, 100
tenor clef, 9
Theatre Monnaie, Brussels, 72, 75
Theatre Royal, Hobart, 86
Third Symphony (Bax), 10
Third Symphony (Brahms), 23
Third Symphony (Sibelius), 100
Third Symphony (Still), 51
The Threepenny Opera (Brecht/Weill), 79
Till Eulenspiegel (Strauss), 95–6
Times, 84–5
timpani, 8, 10, 28
Tippett, Sir Michael, 87
  Fourth Symphony, 88
  Midsummer Marriage, 86–8
tone, 112
tone poem, 112
tone row, 112
Torbay Male Voice Choir, 48
Toscanini, Arturo, xi, 19, 34
trade union movement, 1, 44
transposing instruments, 8–9
transposition, 112
La traviata (Verdi), 54, 64, 96
Treatise on Instrumentation (Berlioz/Strauss), 7, 42

Index

tremolo, 9, 113
trio, 112
Tristan und Isolde (Wagner), 5
tromba, 112
trombone, 8, 9
Trombone Concerto (Sirocco), 10
trumpet, 8, 9
tuba, 8, 10
tuned drum, 10
Turandot (Puccini), 15
Il turco in Italia (Rossini), 69
Turkish music, 112
Turn of the Screw (Britten), 51, 79, 80, 82

Unfinished Symphony (Schubert), 23
upbeat, 112
Ur-text, 112
Ustinov, Peter, 85

valse, 103
Van Allan, Richard, 86
van Dieren, Bernard, *The Chinese Symphony*, 71, 73
Varviso, Silvio, 60
Vaughan, Carolyn, 87
Vaughan-Williams, Ralph, 11, 48, 73
　Fourth Symphony, 65
　Job, 94
　Riders to the Sea, 91
　Tallis Fantasia, 97, 107
Verdi, Giuseppe, 10
　Ava Maria, 107
　Falstaff, 20, 55
　Luisa Miller, 68
　Macbeth, 57, 67
　Quatre pezzi sacre, 107
　Requiem, 84
　Rigoletto, 51, 72
　La traviata, 54, 64, 96
vibraphone, 10
vibrato, 9, 112–13
Vier Letzte Lieder (Strauss), 92, 94
Le Villi (Puccini), 83
viola, 8, 9, 29
violin, 8, 11, 28–9
Violin Concerto (Brian), 66
Violin Concerto (Elgar), 24

Violin Concerto (Sibelius), 65
The Visit of the Old Lady (Einem), 77
Vivace, 98, 100
Vivaldi, Antonio, 45
vocal score, 113
Vorspiel, 113

Wagner, Richard, 23, 45, 73
　Beecham's conducting of, 100
　Beethoven's *Choral Symphony*, 11, 42
　as conductor, 43
　on Habeneck, 42
　Liszt's views on conductors, 43
　Der Ring des Nibelungen, 83, 90
　Siegfried Idyll, 30
　singing, 18
　State Opera of South Australia, 90
　Tannhäuser, 66
　Tristan und Isolde, 5
　use of ophicleide, 10
　Wesendock Lieder, 86
The Walk to the Paradise Garden (Delius), 62
Walter, Bruno, xi, 5, 12, 25, 27
waltzes, 39, 101, 103
Warlock, Peter, 70, 71
Weill, Kurt, *The Threepenny Opera*, 79
Welsh National Opera, 54, 79
Werther (Massenet), 67, 82, 96
Wesendock Lieder (Wagner), 86
Westminster Abbey, 59
Wexford Festival, 64–5, 68–9, 73
The Whale (Tavener), 64
whip, 10
wind-machine, 10
Winslade, Glen, 88
Wolf, Hugo, 22–3
women, as conductors, xi, 20–1
Wood, Anne, 49, 50
Wood, Sir Henry, 9
woodwind instruments, 4, 8, 9–10, 28
Wray, Dr. John, 47, 48

Young, Simone, 21, 91

Die Zauberflöte (Mozart), 20, 25, 55, 57, 63–4, 67, 69, 75, 89, 95
Zeffirelli, Franco, 55